Artificial Intelligence

Techniques and Optimization

Dr. G. Kumaresan

*Central University of Tamil Nadu,
Thiruvarur, India*

ISBN 9789355287922   MJP Publishers

All rights reserved   No. 44, Nallathambi Street,
Printed and bound in India   Triplicane, Chennai 600 005

MJP   1734   Publishers, 2025

Publisher :   **C. Janarthanan**

Project Editor :   **C. Ambica**

List of Figures

List of Tables

Preface

"What you have learned is a mere handful; what you haven't learned is the size of the world." - Avvaiyar

Every time I look at the sky at night, I think of it. Every visible star in the sky is a sun. The nearest star to our planet is the Sun. Then, each star has a solar system. It would be possible for a planet like Earth to survive. There are chances of life on those planets. It is scary to think that we are alone in this universe. We are not the only ones who are afraid. We are at a blue dot. We have been living in some corner, not knowing where we are. Where is the end of this universe? I am curious to know how much I learned. But what is unlearned is cosmic in scale. If this is reflected artificially, it is an artificial universe. Similarly, artificial replication of intelligence is called artificial intelligence. Artificial intelligence plays a significant role in solving complex real-world problems in the digital world. This textbook focuses on artificial intelligence techniques and their optimization process. Artificial intelligence optimization speeds up how AI systems handle information and make decisions. This makes them much faster and better at responding to tasks. Additionally, it can solve complicated issues more accurately by optimizing their work, a clear benefit that drives technology progress even further. It makes it much easier for AI systems to be scaled up, which lets them quickly analyze vast amounts of data. Also, these applications can be customized with an unmatched level of accuracy by carefully setting the AI models to meet specific user needs.

This textbook explains how important it is to make systems work better and make them as flexible and adaptable as possible in all areas of artificial intelligence. In addition, this textbook encourages new ideas by making it possible to create intelligent systems that can solve complex problems. This textbook allows people to find answers that can significantly affect society. Based on the current state of the art in this field, this textbook aims to provide updated knowledge on artificial intelligence techniques and optimization with the proper chapters.

Anyone who wants to learn the basics of artificial intelligence should read this book. The author of this book hopes that people will enjoy reading it and get a general idea of the methods and technicalities used in artificial intelligence. Lastly, never believe what other people say; check everything that can be verified, and then make up your own mind. I hope you have as much fun reading this book as I did writing it.

CUTN, Thiruvarur, India   G. Kumaresan

Acknowledgments

The first step in any technological writing assignment is to understand the field sufficiently. I appreciate all the authors of esteemed books, research documentation, and online articles whose valuable contributions have enhanced the literature on artificial intelligence and related disciplines. Their work facilitated my comprehension of the intricate technical minutiae of the topic. Publications and other resource materials were highly beneficial and provided by reputable artificial intelligence providers. I want to express my appreciation to the commissioning editors at MJP Publishers, with whom I collaborated, for their invaluable recommendations and support in ensuring the success of this endeavor. Their professionalism and competence made working with them an exceptional experience.

Special gratitude is extended to those who provided comprehensive comments, which greatly assisted me in improving the clarity of the content presented. Authoring a technical textbook is a time-consuming endeavor that demands meticulous mental focus. As a result of my professional commitments, most of the work had to be completed outside of regular class hours and during holidays in front of my computer at the computer science department at the Central University of Tamilnadu, Thiruvarur. This achievement would have been unattainable without the helping environment I experienced in the computer science department, and I thank all the faculty members, students, research scholars, and non-teaching staff. Their presence consistently rejuvenated me. I express my gratitude to all those who have imparted knowledge in several subfields of computer science, particularly artificial intelligence.

I want to thank all the professors who taught me computer science and related subjects during my studies. Furthermore, I thank all my friends for their invaluable assistance and insightful conversations throughout my tenure at the Central University of Tamilnadu, Thiruvarur. Finally, and certainly not insignificantly, I want to convey my profound and sincere appreciation to my parents, Mr. R. Gopalan and Mrs. G. Ganambal, who have served as a very influential and motivating force. I am grateful to my brother, sisters, brothers-in-law, nephews, and nieces for their unwavering understanding, affection, and moral support throughout life. At last, I express my gratitude to all my well-wishers who provided direct or indirect assistance while writing this book.

Table of Contents

Chapter 1

Introduction to Artificial Intelligence

1.1   Goal of the Chapter

This chapter goal is to explore the field of artificial intelligence. It is challenging for newcomers to comprehend the theory behind artificial intelligence. Furthermore, they are still determining where to begin or which issues are most suited for employing artificial intelligence techniques and resources. This chapter aims to provide beginners with a foundational understanding of artificial intelligence. It begins with an introduction before offering a trip through this field's history.

1.2   Introduction

For almost 250 million years, we have been living on this Earth, overcoming many challenges of nature. The main reason for this is the planets and sub-planets around the Earth. For example, the moon, a sub-planet of the Earth, protects us due to its gravitational force, which stops the high-speed rotation of the Earth. The other planet, Jupiter, defends the Earth by attracting more meteors that might hit the Earth. Thus, nature protects us with the help of other planets. Similarly, varieties of technologies have been invented and are being used. However, like humans, *Artificial Intelligence* technologies are identical to natural environments. Artificial intelligence systems are capable of solving many complex issues. But these require optimal solutions, which come from intelligence. If not, artificial intelligence won't accomplish its goals. Artificial intelligence technologies are, therefore, necessary to achieve a state of harmony with nature. We generally refer to ourselves as Homo sapiens since we value intelligence so highly. We have spent many years figuring out how we think—how a small amount of matter can see, comprehend, anticipate, and control a world that is considerably more complex and vast than itself. Artificial intelligence goes beyond that in that it aims to create and comprehend sentient beings. When artificial intelligence was first developed, scientists believed that creating machines with the ability to reason using a database of facts would be a natural next step, which was the application of logical principles and data to conclude in the deductive reasoning method of artificial intelligence. Put another way, reasoning using logic aims to arrive at provably sound logical conclusions from a foundation of well-established hypotheses. Nevertheless, it was quickly discovered that this method of approaching artificial intelligence needed to be revised for something more than logical deduction. Much of human intellect stems from *Empirical Knowledge* from daily experiences that validate gut instincts. Provably accurate conclusions are frequently sacrificed to get non-obvious conclusions. Approaches based on data-driven practical learning quickly emerged. Rather than assuming pre-defined hypotheses, data instances supply the evidence required to construct hypotheses and draw conclusions from them. In 1997, IBM's computer program *Deep Blue* defeated the world chess champion, Gary Kasparov. That was when most people paid serious attention to artificial intelligence, a rapidly developing branch of computer science. AI is one of the most recent areas of engineering and science. Scientists from other fields are the most interested in using AI. Artificial intelligence currently includes a wide range of subfields, from *Learning* and *Perception* to more specialized tasks like playing chess, proving theorems in mathematics, creating poetry, operating a car in a congested area, and detecting illnesses. AI is a general field that applies to every intellectual work.

The structure of this chapter is as follows: The historical perspective of artificial intelligence is covered in the next section. Section 1.4 discusses generic types of artificial intelligence and the Turing test. In Sections 1.5 and 1.6, respectively, the concepts of an agent and environment—essential to artificial intelligence—are introduced. In Section 1.7, learning system types are covered. Section 1.8 discusses neural network techniques in artificial intelligence. Section 1.9 provides a summary of this chapter.

1.3 Historical Perspective

The basis of artificial intelligence was laid between 400 BC and the 18th century. The first idea is task automation, which refers to computers that do computations automatically and operate autonomously without human assistance. For example, around 400 BC, the Greek mechanic Archytas of Tarentum created the first mechanical pigeon that could fly on its own and cover a distance of 200 meters using steam power. After that, in the latter part of the 1490s, Leonardo da Vinci created several machines and robots that automated laborious and specific activities. Charles Babbage, the inventor of computers, also called the analytical engine, invented them in 1837, during the Industrial Revolution and the invention of machinery. The 1940s and 1950s saw the emergence of AI concepts. Because of the idea of acting machines, renowned mathematician Alan Turing is one of the motivators of artificial intelligence (additional information is provided in Section 1.4.1). A Turing test theory was developed to see if a machine could be as intelligent as a person [Tur50]. After that, the first artificial intelligence program that could replicate some features of human intellect appeared in the late 1950s. That artificial intelligence program could demonstrate geometric theorems, solve algebraic issues, and acquire new knowledge. John McCarthy, considered the father of AI and a pioneer of artificial intelligence at the Massachusetts Institute of Technology (MIT), was the one who first used the term artificial intelligence.

The creation of computer programs that carry out tasks currently completed most satisfactorily by humans is what Marvin Minsky termed artificial intelligence. Due to this, they need higher-order cognitive functions, including critical thinking, memory organizing, and perceptual learning [Min61]. The discipline's origins are credited to the Dartmouth College summer conference of 1956. It is essential to note that the workshop, rather than the conference, was a huge success. Based on improvements in formal logic, only six people continued with the work, including McCarthy and Minsky. The early 1960s saw a decline in the popularity of technology, despite its attractiveness and promise [Law63]. Because machines had extremely little memory, using computer language was challenging. Nonetheless, some groundwork for problem-solving

Table 1.1: AI Historical Viewpoint

Timeline	Engagements
400 BC	Mechanical Pigeon Invented
Later Part of 1490s	Automated Robots
1837	First General Mechanical Computer Invented
1940s to 1950s	Emergence of AI Concepts
1960s to 1970s	In the Beginning Stages of Growth
1980s	The Winter of AI & Expert Systems
1990s	Revival and emergence of ML
2000s	The Start of Generative AI
2010s	The Development of Artificial Intelligence
2020s	Advancements in Generative AI Expand Boundaries

techniques, including solution trees, was already in place. For example, a logic theorist could create machine programs to prove mathematical theorems as early as 1956, thanks to a data processing language. Economist and sociologist Herbert Simon predicted in 1957 that artificial intelligence would defeat a human in chess within the next ten years, but AI only faced its first winter. Early in the 1970s, artificial intelligence was met with skepticism and decreased investment because of unrealistic expectations and the state of technology at the time. But in the 1980s, expert systems—replicating human expert decision-making capabilities in particular domains—saw a revival. Subsequently, the 1990s and 2000s saw the dawn of the neural network era. *Deep Learning* and *Neural Networks* allow machines to identify patterns and handle massive datasets quickly. In the 1990s, algorithms that could outsmart humans at intricate board games were also developed. The 1997 victory of IBM's Deep Blue over chess champion Garry Kasparov was a significant turning point (Cf. Section 1.2). The current era of artificial intelligence began in 2010 due to substantial investments made in the field by digital behemoths like Google, Amazon, and Apple. These days, voice assistants, tailored shopping experiences, stock market trend prediction, and intricate scientific research are all made possible by artificial intelligence algorithms. Table 1.1 summarizes the historical perspectives on AI. The potential for AI to transform industries and impact human history is bright, especially with the emergence of quantum computing and increasingly complex algorithms. Reaffirmed promises and occasionally imagined worries obstruct a dispassionate comprehension of the phenomena. A brief review of the discipline's past can assist in framing the present discussions.

1.4   Intelligence in General

The subfield of artificial intelligence, known as *Artificial General Intelligence*, or AGI, deals with highly autonomous systems that can learn, comprehend, and apply information in various contexts and domains, much like human intelligence. AGI aims to build computers capable of complex cognitive activities, reasoning, natural language understanding, situational adaptation, and experience-based learning. The ability of AGI to transfer knowledge and skills between domains, demonstrating a degree of versatility and adaptability comparable to human intellect, sets it apart from more constrained or specialized artificial intelligence systems. Artificial general intelligence aims to imitate human perception, learning, memory, reasoning, and decision-making, among other cognitive functions [GP07]. To mimic a tiny child's reasoning ability, Simon, Shaw, and Newell created a general-purpose problem-solving program in 1959. Unfortunately, most of these systems haven't been able to advance past basic toy settings [NSS59]. Developing AGI raises enormous problems owing to the difficulty of mimicking human intelligence. It necessitates developments in several fields, including computer vision, robotics, natural language processing, machine learning, and cognitive science. AI research and organizations aim to create AGI to address complex issues, including automation, scientific research, medicine, and even the arts. Notably, AGI is still primarily an aspirational aim and a current study and development topic. Although significant advancements have been made in specific AI fields, obtaining AGI on par with more advanced human intelligence is a challenging and continuous project. However, given the failure of general-purpose systems, one may wonder what the ultimate objective of general-purpose artificial intelligence could be. The Turing test was the first to articulate this goal openly.

1.4.1   Alan Turing Test

In artificial intelligence, a *Turing Test* is a research technique used to evaluate whether a computer can think similarly to a human. The test was named after the English mathematician Alan Turing, who developed *Machine Learning* in the 1940s and 1950s. Turing claimed that the ability of a machine to mimic human behavior under specific conditions qualifies it as artificial intelligence. The original Turing test, often called the imitation game, requires three terminals, each physically isolated from the other two. A computer operates one terminal, while humans use the other two. The test's questioner is one of the humans, and the test's respondent is the other human plus the computer. In keeping with a predefined framework and context, the questioner poses questions to the respondents regarding a particular subject. After a predefined period of questions, the questioner is asked to judge which respondent is a human or a computer. The test is conducted several times. Suppose the questioner believes the computer to be just as human as the response, and the machine accurately predicts the answer in 50% or less of test runs. In that case, the computer is considered to have artificial intelligence [Moo03]. Figure 1.1 shows an example of a typical Turing test. The Turing Test has been criticized over time, in part because, in the past, the questions' subject matter had to be limited for a machine to exhibit intelligence comparable to that of a human. A computer could only obtain a high score for an extended period if the questions were designed to allow for a binary

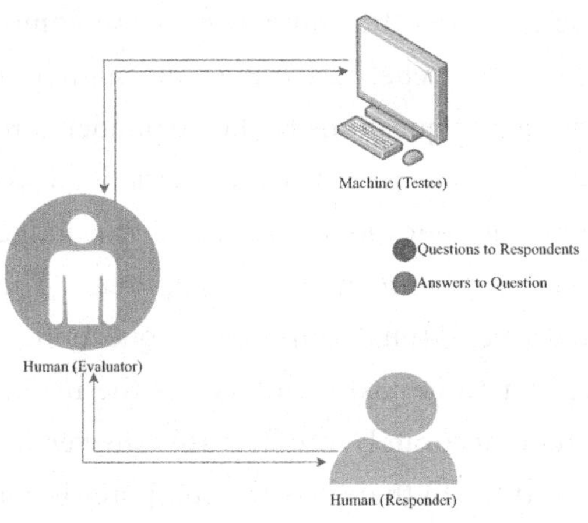

Figure 1.1: An Example of a Typical Turing Test

response of yes or no, or if they pertained to a specific field of knowledge. When questions were open-ended and required conversational answers, the likelihood of the computer program fooling the asker was reduced. For many scientists, the question of a machine's ability to pass the Turing test is no longer relevant. The proper focus should be on improving the effectiveness and naturalness of human-machine interaction—for instance, by employing a conversational interface—rather than convincing people they are chatting with a person rather than a computer program. Without question, the Turing test represents the technological apex. However, there is a need to work extra hard to pass the Turing Test without changing accepted notions of intelligence.

1.5   Agent Approach

Agent-based AI, also called *Intelligent Agents* or *Artificial Intelligence Agents*, gained some attraction in the 1990s. Like human agents, these are highly developed software systems that carry out particular tasks independently. It can interact with its surroundings to accomplish a specific collection of goals. Entities that employ *Sensors* to sense their environments, form decisions, and use *Actuators* to carry out their actions are known as intelligent agents. A robot, machine, human, animal, or any combination could be an intelligent agent. A camera, rain sensor, or nose could be the sensor that senses the surroundings. After analyzing this data, the intelligent agent chooses how to proceed. The action could include locating the closest pizza place, stopping a sprinkler system, or saving a movie. The component that initiates action is the actuator. Intelligent agents make real-time decisions, and their success and error rates differ. Reacting to its surroundings is the aim of an intelligent agent. Numerous facets of daily life involve intelligent agents, such as refrigerators that use temperature sensing to determine when more cooling is required. When smoke is detected, smoke detectors begin to sound an alarm. An additional example of an intelligent agent is a dog that barks when a stranger approaches the door. Self-driving cars and the SpaceX Dragon spacecraft are examples of complex intelligent agents. These intelligent agents gather data from numerous sensors, decide in real-time, and modify their course of action accordingly. Intelligent agents can typically adjust to novel circumstances and draw lessons from past encounters. It can also plan, reason, and make decisions based on erroneous or partial knowledge. In addition, they can also monitor their surroundings, spot issues, and act appropriately to resolve them. The concept of agents was first introduced in Minsky's book "Society of Mind." Drawing on ideas from game theory, distributed computing, sociology, psychology, and other fields, it has grown into a complex field with many related technologies, including NetLogo, JADE, FIPA, and many more [Min88]. Agent-based AI is incredibly less widely used, given all those advantages. Most AI-related research efforts have focused on machine learning, which is the reason. Generally speaking, AI agents still lack an assassin application field. This should be connected to the *Internet of Things* or *IoT* because, in the latter case, any centralized solution won't be scalable, and any minor issue could bring down the ecosystem as a whole. In contrast, agents' overall performance tends to degrade gracefully in the former case. AI agents are generally intended to be more adaptive, versatile, and self-sufficient than conventional computer programs. They have many uses, including robotics, natural language processing, autonomous cars, etc. They can carry out tasks and make decisions that resemble human intelligence. In artificial intelligence, the environment is crucial to an agent's performance and is detailed in Section 1.6.

1.6   Some Environment Types

Artificial intelligence allows for an infinite variety of environments. Furthermore, different environments correspond to different kinds of issues. Every setting is distinct from the others. When an AI agent can directly and fully witness the state of the environment at any one time, that environment is said to be *Fully Observable*, which implies that the representative has access to all pertinent data, including the data required for decision-making. The *Chess* Board, where a player can always see all their pieces, their opponent's pieces, and the board's squares, is the best example of this environment. Conversely, a *Partially Observable* environment is one in which the AI agent cannot directly witness the entirety of the environment. In this situation, the agent might only have access to limited environmental data, which could complicate decision-making. AI agents frequently employ strategies like belief states and memory to preserve and update their understanding of the environment over time in partially observable situations, which enables individuals to make secure decisions even in the face of incomplete knowledge. *Driving* a car is one example of this environment. When operating a vehicle, one can only see limited areas and cannot see around the corner. An environment

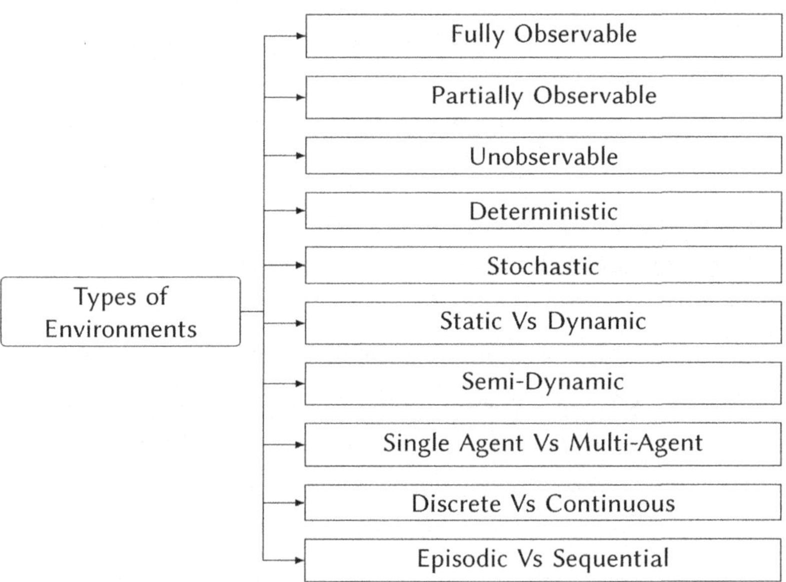

Figure 1.2: Types of AI Environments

is considered *Unobservable* if an agent receives no

information.

The university classroom listening lesson for *Deaf* students illustrates this environment. But since they are uncommon, these kinds of situations are only sometimes thought of as environments. Let's say an agent repeatedly performs the same action in the same state. In the end, it will always produce the same results. This kind of setting is called a *Deterministic* environment, which is distinct and unfeasible for random events. An illustration of this kind of environment is when two hydrogen atoms always join with an oxygen atom to form *Water*. That state and activity will never yield anything other than water. In contrast, random events can occur in *Stochastic* environments. This implies that the next state or result cannot be precisely predicted for a given current state and the action taken by the agent. Furthermore, this is sometimes called the *Markov Decision Process*. Playing in a *Soccer* match is the best way to experience this environment. If the agent kicks the ball in a specific direction, other players may or may not stop it, and player movement can change the soccer field in a number of different ways. Most real-life situations are stochastic because of the intricacy of billions of environmental factors and extra agents. In a *Static* environment, nothing changes in the settings while the agent deliberates on a task. Thus, an agent is free to consider the problem for as long as they wish if efficiency is not required for performance. An example of a static environment is when a dry cleaner robot cleans a room, keeping the space static throughout the process. The *Dynamic* environment will keep evolving while the agent thinks. The tasks surrounding soccer players do not stop when they feel they do, even when they are evaluating the locations of other players in an attempt to score a goal. A player from the other team will dart in and seize the ball. When the environment does not alter as the agent thinks, but the agent's performance score does, this is referred to as a *Semi-Dynamic* intermediate state. A robot vacuum, for instance, is mainly in a static environment in a house devoid of living things. However, if the robot's efficiency is based on how quickly it completes the cleaning, the longer it takes to decide, the lower its efficiency score becomes. A single-agent environment is one in which a *Single-Agent* handles all of the environment's tasks. Playing tennis against the ball in a single-agent game with just one player best illustrates this scenario.

An environment where multiple agents operate together is called a *Multi-Agent* environment. A football game is one instance of this kind of environment. On the other hand, a *Discrete* environment has a limited quantity of perceptions and actions. A real-world instance of this type of setting is a game of chess, where the number of possible moves on the chessboard is countable. An unlimited number of observations and activities occur in a *Continuous* environment. A multi-agent *Basketball* game is the best real-time illustration of this situation. There are countless options in the surroundings because players' positions are constantly shifting and because there are several angles and speeds at which the ball can be struck toward the basket. An *Episodic* environment without any connection to the subsequent state is one in which every state exists independently of the others. An online bot that responds to one query, then another, and so on, is the best illustration of this kind of environment. Each episode is, therefore, a single episode. Finally, in a *Sequential* environment, the action taken in one state determines the next. Hence, an agent's current actions can alter every future state of the environment. Playing tennis is the ideal illustration of this kind of setting. After watching the opponent's shot, the player responds state by state. To help you understand better, Figure 1.2 shows different types of AI environments.

1.7   Learning in Artificial Intelligence

As per the renowned Harvard psychologist William James, the term "learning" is relatively well-defined. Basically, learning is becoming more proficient at a task through experience [Jam07]. AI agents are computer programs that function in different environments, taking information from those environments and using it to accomplish distinct objectives. "If a computer program's performance at tasks in T, as measured by P, improves with experience E, then it is said to learn from experience E concerning some class of tasks in T and performance measure P," states Tom M. Mitchell's definition [Mit79]. Thus, learning truly only makes sense about a specific goal. An agent handles the learning process in AI. In an artificial intelligence setting, there are various kinds of learning agents. First, static agents are characterized by constants that remain the same over time. The goal of a multi-core central processing unit model would be to look into how operational performance changes as the number of cores increases for different input and output bandwidths. Each core would have fixed operating characteristics. Learning agents aren't *Static Agents.*

On the other hand, some agents' properties vary while the model is executed. Programming an *Economic Agent* in a financial model with optional trade strategies is possible. Its choice of trade tactics may differ as it gets more data if it keeps track of its transactions, including clients, items, and pricing. These agents are called learning agents because they learn to choose the *Optimal* option among multiple possible answers by retaining and utilizing data. An agent may develop brand-new trading strategies or adopt creative strategies from other agencies. Transformations in a set of operational properties, like a genome, that impact performance as determined by a fitness metric are usually the source of innovation. A population of agents will evolve due to the capacity to create improved or novel trading strategies to increase performance and some form of natural selection that removes underperforming individuals. Due to their innovative and novel reactions, these agents are also called learning agents. Section 1.7.1 explains a few common learning types.

1.7.1 Different Learning Types

Learning is one of the crucial methods in artificial intelligence to enhance an agent's components. These advancements come with several obstacles, such as optimization and many more. Learning is categorized into five basic groups based on the methods and approaches depicted in Figure 1.3. The following sections 1.7.2 to 1.7.6 explain its learning types.

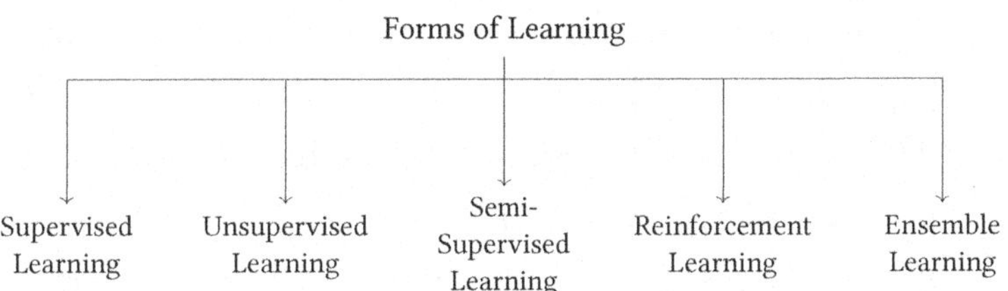

Figure 1.3: Various Forms of Learning

1.7.2 Supervised Learning

Supervised learning techniques are one of the vital subcategories of ML and AI. It trains algorithms to identify data or predict outcomes accurately using labeled datasets. The model may learn over time because the training dataset contains inputs and accurate outputs. The learning process gauges its accuracy through the loss function and adjusts until the error is suitably reduced. Classification and *Regression* are two main categories of data mining challenges that fall under the umbrella of supervised learning [CCD]. The *Classification* applies an algorithm to accurately place test data into distinct categories. It identifies different entities in the dataset and makes an effort to make recommendations on the proper definition or labeling of those things. In order to comprehend the link between dependent and independent variables, regression analysis is utilized. It is frequently used to forecast things like sales income for a particular company. As an example of *Supervised Learning*, let's say you have data from healthy, normal patients, and you need to create a model that categorizes patients as such. In this instance, it is known that the subject is either normal or a patient. The numerous well-liked applications listed one by one demonstrate these types of learning: The *Ad-Popularity* application is where it all starts. Choosing effective advertisements is frequently a supervised learning process. When you visit the Internet, many advertisements exist because the learning algorithm deems them somewhat popular. Furthermore, a trained algorithm that determines when the ad and placement match is primarily responsible for its order on a particular website or about a specific search query you happen to be typing into a search engine. Spam categorization is an additional program that filters some unsolicited messages. You have undoubtedly encountered spam filters if you use one of the newer email services. A supervised learning system underlies that *Spam Filter.* These systems are designed to recognize a harmful email before it is sent and classify it as spam, allowing users to utilize it without interruption. Many of these also exhibit behaviors that will enable the user to give the system new labels, and the system picks up on the user's preferences. Furthermore, a supervised learning algorithm taught to recognize your face has used a *Face Recognition* program. A system that detects faces in an image and makes educated estimates about who is in it is supervised. Despite having several layers that find and then see faces, it is still under observation.

1.7.3 Unsupervised Learning

An unsupervised learning algorithm's foundation is the input dataset distribution using an unidentified underlying statistical distribution. *Unsupervised Learning* techniques aim to discover the true nature of this distribution. It needs to define what a cluster or group is to search the data for clusters or groups. These algorithms are similar to the self-sufficient cats in machine learning [HW62]; they can solve problems without external guidance. The *K-Means* clustering technique is one instance of an unsupervised algorithm. This algorithm resembles a cat, which enjoys assembling objects into groups. It clusters many data points according to how similar they are. The algorithm may group these data points because they all want to chase laser pointers. *Principal Component Analysis* is an additional unsupervised technique. This algorithm simplifies things, much like a cat. It distills much-complicated information down to what's most important. We can condense this data to only a few essential characteristics, including size, color, and material, since it may indicate that it is all about cat toys. The *Auto-Encoder* algorithm is similar to a cat that enjoys playing hide-and-seek. It attempts to conceal a large amount of information in a condensed area. It then attempts to use less space to recover the original data. Even though these unsupervised algorithms don't require human supervision, they can do some amazing things independently. These algorithms can recognize patterns and make sense of data without human intervention, like a cat can navigate a house independently. Because unsupervised learning can automatically find structure in data, it is beneficial in exploratory analysis. When human judgment cannot identify patterns in the data, unsupervised learning can offer a preliminary understanding that can be applied to test specific theories.

1.7.4 Semi-Supervised Learning

Learning that is semi-supervised combines the benefits of unsupervised and supervised learning. Using all available data is the primary goal of *Semi-Supervised* learning, focusing exclusively on labeled data instead of supervised learning. In an unsupervised learning technique, similar data is first clustered. It then assists in marking the unlabeled data to create labeled data because acquiring labeled data is generally more costly than unlabeled data. It is also helpful when getting labeled data takes a long time, costs money, or calls for specific expertise [ZG22]. For example, semi-supervised learning is like going on a field trip with your computer. Your computer might not spend the entire day in a classroom studying textbooks; instead, it might take a break, walk outside, and learn from its experiences. This technique helps your computer recognize patterns and make inferences without having you provide labeled data for every instance. A small number of examples are all that the computer needs to get going; the rest will come from its own experiences. Through self-observation, the computer might pick up knowledge and insights it otherwise wouldn't have. It is comparable to a global tour with a guide. Semi-supervised machine learning effectively gives robots more intelligence and improves their ability to understand their surroundings. Large-scale image labeling in *Computer Vision* can also be problematic. Still, limited quantities of photos are labeled. In that case, a semi-supervised learning model can be taught to identify *Patterns* in the images, which it can then use to classify the other photos in the unlabeled dataset. Semi-supervised learning is a valuable and significant technique within machine learning, a subset of artificial intelligence, to optimize the use of labeled and unlabeled data.

1.7.5   Reinforcement Learning

Reinforcement learning differs from supervised learning because it does not require the presentation of labeled input and output pairs or the explicit correction of inferior actions. Many reinforcement learning algorithms work with dynamic programming, which means they know how to make exact decisions. This means that the environment is usually a Markov decision process [VW12]. When AI systems must learn to make decisions or follow specific steps to accomplish a task, *Reinforcement Learning* (RL) is a crucial training tool. In this type of machine learning, an agent gradually gains the ability to interact with its environment to maximize total reward. RL draws inspiration from behavioral psychology and focuses on teaching practitioners how to solve problems through *Trial and Error*, that is, by making numerous attempts until one succeeds or gives up [Cam60]. An AI agent in RL picks up knowledge by interacting with its surroundings. The environment reacts to the agent's behavior by offering rewards and new states. This participatory method is similar to how people and animals pick up new skills through trial, error, and feedback. The agent seeks to acquire a policy, or action selection method, that optimizes its cumulative reward. *Reward* systems give input on how desirable an agent's activities are. The trade-off between *Exploration* and *Exploitation* is one of the primary issues in RL. In addition to using established actions that provide larger rewards, the agent must experiment with novel actions to discover better tactics. Finding the ideal balance is essential to learning effectively. The main objective of reinforcement learning is to find the optimal strategy that maximizes the expected total reward. To accomplish this goal, the agent gains knowledge of the appropriate course of action in various scenarios. Learning value actions are included in RL in addition to learning concepts. Value functions calculate the expected total reward for a particular state or state-action combination. Agents can make wise selections with the aid of these evaluations. Problems with judgments made over time or in sequences are well suited for reinforcement learning, which makes reinforcement learning perfect for applications such as recommendation systems, gaming, robotics, autonomous driving, and more. RL can handle scenarios in which rewards could be delayed and allows the agent to assign the right actions to rewards even if they happened a few steps earlier. In practical terms, how does AI, in a real-time setting, learn from its successes and failures, and how do humans pick up and remember knowledge? Your head lacks the hard drive necessary to store your acquired knowledge. That biological matrix, which is made up of signals and inducible inter-forces, reflects everything you've learned, including memories, preferences, and attitudes, as well as your billions of *Neurons* with their trillions of connections and trillions of trillions of *Pattern Firings*. You access, use, and regenerate this energy in a huge parallel pattern every instant. Neurons distinct to your recollections—your grandmother's face, the scent of a rose—do not keep your specific experiences. In holographic mode, they are shared by millions of neurons and stored as a firing pattern, similar to how a portion of a holographic image shows multiple images depending on the angle at which it is viewed. The strength of a signal that a neuron can send to thousands of other neurons or the strength with which it can send a signal to those other neurons, is determined by the minute but persistent variations in neurotransmitter concentrations, which occur cell by cell. It pays attention to these neurons' impulses. There is also evidence that a certain neuron can talk to the exact distal neuronal sequence to receive dendrites from its nerve and that neurons can grow and change slowly, changing how neurons connect with each other. For instance, if you wrongly believe that Radhakrishnan was the first President of India and then correct yourself, your mental association between Rajendra Prasad and the First President will get stronger over time. Although we prefer to believe that the things we store are absolutes, they are only mental simplifications. AI mimics this *Biological Matrix* on a much smaller scale and with simpler interconnected patterns utilizing regular mathematical matrices, notably true of ML and replication patterns based on *Artificial Neural Networks*. The current signal intensity of hypothetical neurons in one layer related to neurons in adjacent layers is represented by several thousand values in each matrix. Similar bodies of matrices can hold values that reduce the sensitivity of those earlier connection-strength neurons. In contrast, incorrect conduct leads the AI in the opposite direction, unsystematically looking for the best outcomes. The more the AI shifts from wrong to right behavior, the more previous differential link strengths move in the present direction. Similar to how people get accustomed to particular habits, values become more difficult to modify as answers are received on a given activity more correctly. Another major problem with this kind of learning is how the AI obtains feedback on whether or not it did something correctly. It must communicate with a system, assess its accuracy, and adjust. *Deep Reinforcement Learning*, which enables AI agents to learn complicated behaviors and judge high-dimensional inputs like images and audio, combines reinforcement learning with *Deep Neural Networks*. Applications for reinforcement learning include teaching self-driving cars to navigate intricate landscapes, streamlining industrial processes, enabling non-human players to play games like Go versus chess, and programming robots to carry out tasks.

1.7.6   Ensemble Learning

Ensemble Learning, or EL, is a form of machine learning that entails merging predictions from different models to enhance overall performance and generalization [Don+20]. These objectives can be accomplished using algorithms such as *Bagging*, *Boosting*, and *Random Forest*. The primary goal of this technique is to minimize the errors that may be present in the separate models. Additionally, using the advantages of many models, EL enhances the overall performance of the learning system. This strategy improves precision and offers adaptability when dealing with uncertainties in the data. Also, it provides more resilient and dependable predictions. Consider a precise real-time scenario: imagine you are a film director who has produced a short film about a significant and captivating subject. Now, you want to gather initial input, specifically ratings, on the movie before its release. What are all the potential methods by which you can accomplish that? Soliciting your friends' opinions to evaluate the film may not be advisable since some of them may purposefully provide inflated ratings due to your relationship. An alternative approach might involve soliciting evaluations of the film from seven of your coworkers. However, this is also unfavorable as they may need more expertise. What if we solicit the opinions of 100 individuals to assess the quality of the film? Among them, there may be individuals who are:

- Your friends.
- Others who are your coworkers.
- Even others who are strangers.

A heterogeneous group is more likely to make superior selections than solitary individuals. ML diversification is accomplished using ensemble learning, a methodology that combines simple methods such as *Max Voting*, *Averaging*, and *Weighted Averages* to create a powerful approach. Max voting involves employing several techniques to produce predictions for each data point. The forecasts of each model are aggregated as a collective vote. The majority of votes determine the final predictions. For instance, if we have five individuals labeled as $m_1=6$, $m_2=7$, $m_3=6$, $m_4=7$, and $m_5=7$, each representing distinct models, we must utilize the max voting strategy to make a prediction. The ultimate prediction is 7, corresponding to most individuals' highest rating. The averaging method involves calculating the average estimates from all the models, which is then utilized to generate the final prediction. Let's consider the same example: the total amount of all the ratings is 33, and the average rating is 6.6, the final predicted rating. Weighted average involves assigning various weights to each model and expands the concept of averaging. The ultimate prediction rating is 4.1, calculated as the sum of $(6 \times 0.12) + (7 \times 0.13) + (6 \times 0.12) + (7 \times 0.12) + (7 \times 0.13)$. Three categories of ensemble classifiers exist bagging, boosting, and random forest. Bagging generates heterogeneous subsets of the training data, trains multiple models in parallel, and computes the average of their predictions. Random Forests are a widely used illustration. Boosting, however, involves constructing a series of models, with each model rectifying the mistakes made by the previous one. Well-known algorithms such as *AdaBoost* and *Gradient Boosting* adhere to this methodology. An important issue arises from the need for diversity in the ensemble when models are trained individually or in a sequence without considering their interactions. Diversity can be enhanced by utilizing *Neural Networks*, which will be further discussed in the subsequent Section 1.8.

1.8 Neural Networks

Neural networks, which draw inspiration from the structure and function of the human brain, are the foundation of modern AI. They consist of networked nodes called *Neurons* that communicate with one another by sending signals and processing information. Without explicit programming, neural networks can learn from data and generate predictions. *Backpropagation* is a technique commonly used in neural network training that minimizes the error between the predicted and actual output by varying the weights of the connections between neurons. *Neural Networks* can be trained to generate predictions on fresh data [Cha18]. For instance, to forecast whether a new image contains a cat, one can train a neural network to detect photos of cats. Consider a neural network that has been taught to identify cat photos. Each neuron in the input layer analyses a fresh image sent into the neural network and then transmits a signal to the neurons in the subsequent layer. After processing the signals from the input layer, the neurons in the following layer send signals to the layer afterward. This process continues until the last neuron layer produces an output signal. The output signal of the previous layer of neurons represents the neural network's prediction. For instance, the output signal for a neural network that predicts whether or not a cat is present in an image will be a number between 0 and 1. The neural network is more confident that a cat is in the picture if the value is closer to 1. One of its main advantages is neural networks' ability to learn from complex and non-linear input. Because of this, they are well suited for *Machine Translation*, *Image Recognition*, and *Natural Language Processing*, among many others.

1.9 Summary

With cutting-edge technical progress, artificial intelligence is transforming many facets of our lives. First, we talked about artificial intelligence and other concepts that are relevant to the topic. The historical view of artificial intelligence has since emerged, and its future significance is recognized. The Turing test and general intelligence were then considered. It was observed that intelligence was necessary to handle complicated situations without altering the definitions of intelligence. Agents and a few different environmental types are also taken into consideration. The essentials of learning were discussed, along with their significant varieties. Furthermore, the given neural network model resembles these learning techniques.

1.9.1 Multiple Choice Questions

Exercise 1: Which computer chess program defeated world champion Gary Kasparov in 1997?

 a)   b) Battle c) Deep d) Houdini
  Komodo   Chess   Blue

Exercise 2: Who is the father of Artificial Intelligence?

 a) Alan Turing   b) Charles Babbage

 c) John McCarthy   d) Archytas of Tarentum

Exercise 3: Which tool is necessary for observing in the environment?

 a) Sensors b) Bluetooth c) Actuators d) Infrared

Exercise 4: Which tool is necessary for acting in the environment?

 a) Sensors b) Bluetooth c) Actuators d) Infrared

Exercise 5: What kind of environment does a crossword puzzle belong in?

a) Dynamic   b) Static   c) Discrete   d) Sequential

Exercise 6: Select the option that does not fall under any learning category from the list below.

a) Supervised Learning   b) Semi-Unsupervised Learning

c) Reinforcement Learning   d) Unsupervised Learning

Exercise 7: Determine the kind of learning that uses labeled training data.

a) Supervised Learning   b) Semi-Supervised Learning

c) Reinforcement Learning   d) Unsupervised Learning

1.9.2   Short Answer Type Questions

1. Why is artificial intelligence necessary for our everyday lives?

2. What are thinking machines, and how do they work?

3. What is the purpose of artificial intelligence in general?

4. What is the Turing test used to motivate AI researchers?

5. What benefits may intelligent agents provide to humans?

6. Will all AI environments use the Markov decision process?

7. What benefits may data mining offer supervised learning?

8. Will a neural network be used in reinforcement learning?

1.9.3   Long Answer Type Questions

1. Describe the several historical stances on artificial intelligence.

2. Why do agents matter?   Give a thorough explanation of intelligent agents.

3. Enumerate the attributes of the environment with artificial intelligence.

4. Provide relevant examples to illustrate the various forms of machine learning.

Chapter 2

State Space Search to Find Solutions

2.1 Goal of the Chapter

This chapter aims to solve a given problem for artificial intelligence in a state-space search environment. One of AI's most significant operational responsibilities is search, which is utilized to find solutions in challenging situations. Many AI issues are easily represented as state spaces; resolving them requires investigating the state space and figuring out the correct answers. The following sections provide an introduction and then different search techniques.

2.2   Introduction

The AI *Search Agent* has explored every avenue to reach
the objective and every potential result. State space is
necessary for an AI agent to accomplish this objective. A
State Space contains all the mathematically represented
problems the search method uses as potential states. A
set of variables represents each state in the state space.
To determine a sequence of events known as states, the
state space representation first defines initial and goal
states. A state could be the starting point, the end state,
or any other state resulting from combining rules from
different states. Space typically refers to the complete
set of all possible states in the AI issue. By using the
best rules that traverse the space of all possible states,
this type of approach advances from the initial state to
the target state. Typically, a tree-like structure serves
as a representation of a problem. The *Search Tree*'s root
node, where the tree begins, represents the original state,
which explains how each path cost—an activity sequence
that links the starting node to the finishing node—assigns
a cost value. Of all the options, the best one has the
lowest cost. Furthermore, the following is how the search

steps in State Space Search operate: Setting the initial state to the current state is the first step in initializing the search and determining whether the current state is desired following the initialization stage. Finally, stop the procedure and return the outcome if the current state is a *Goal State*. On the other hand, if it is not the goal state, produce the set of states feasible to achieve from the current state. These states are also referred to as successor states. In addition, determine whether each successor state has been visited before. Then, bypass a state if it has previously been examined and add it to the list of states that need to be seen if it has yet to be seen. After that, set the subsequent state in the queue as active, determine whether it is a goal state, and return the outcome if the target state is located. If not, carry out the preceding action until you find the target state or have explored every state. Furthermore, they return without a solution if they have tried every feasible state. The problem determines the algorithm's precise implementation specifics. Furthermore, the *Data Structures* employed to record the states and track the search also affect how well the algorithm performs [LV12]. The size of the state space has a significant impact on the search algorithm's efficiency. Selecting the right *Search Strategy* and representation is critical to search the state space efficiently.

2.3   Uninformed Search

In AI, an *Uninformed Search* is a method where the machine attempts to find every conceivable combination of answers before selecting the *Optimal* solution. The system must investigate every potential solution without prior knowledge of the objective state or current space. Another name for it is a *Blind Search*. Let's examine a straightforward real-time scenario to grasp an uninformed search better. Assume, for illustration, that we have created a computer program to retrieve a password from a secure system. There will be eight digits in the *Password*. The question now is, how can we solve this by figuring out the system's exact password? The simple answer is to write down every possible eight-digit number combination and attempt to log in with that combination. One combination will be able to log in. The number of combinations is the actual issue in this situation. We already know that the password consists of eight digits. Repeating digits are permitted;

each digit may be any integer between 0 and 9. Since there are ten options for each digit and eight digits, the total number of alternatives will be 10^8. Thus, a billion alternatives exist. Reviewing all these options, even with a powerful computer, takes time. But eventually, it will undoubtedly lead us to the correct answer. It refers to this entire procedure as uninformed searching. The following sections cover some of the fundamental, uninformed search algorithms.

2.3.1   Breadth-First Search

The *Breadth-First Search* (BFS) algorithm is classified as an uninformed search strategy since it never provides any information when attempting to achieve the goal state. This graph traversal technique visits every vertex at a level before going on to the next, exploring a graph's vertices in *Breadth-First Order*. Each vertex is tagged as seen and added to a queue, which begins at the root node or any other arbitrary node. Typically, the *First-In-First-Out* queue data structure can be used to implement it. Finding the shortest path between two nodes is a popular application of BFS. This algorithm offers more methods for utilizing the many available paths [Nil82].

Let's now examine the technical workings of the BFS algorithm. Put the root node or the active working node in the queue first. We now need to determine if the queue is empty. Find all of the current working node's successors, child nodes, and unvisited nodes, add them to the queue, and get the output sequence if the queue is not empty. *Dequeue* the node that is presently operating concurrently. Once the queue is empty, designate the node that appears first as the active working node and continue the procedure. Ultimately, the output sequence is produced, such as ABSCGDEHF and more. The figure 2.1 depicts a general breakdown of BFS working methods. Three criteria were used to evaluate the algorithm's

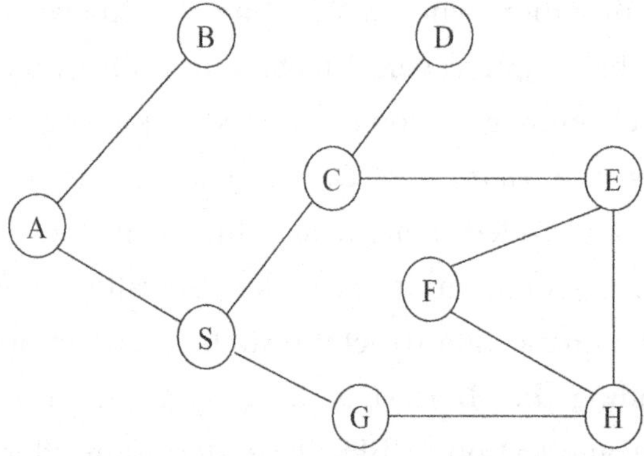

Figure 2.1: General Breakdown of Breadth-First Search

performance: *Completeness*, *Optimality*, and *Time and Space Complexity*. For example, BFS is complete since it provides solutions for the first parameter. BFS will only produce the best result for the second parameter when every node has the exact cost. The deeper a tree gets or the higher the search tree level, the more time and *Memory* are needed for complexity and time. Because of this, the BFS algorithm has significant problems with both time and space complexity. Its time complexity is $\mathcal{O}(b^d)$, where b is the number of nodes and d is the graph's search tree's depth. Let's say you're trying to locate a red *Doodad* among several *Boxes* arranged on a table containing various doodads. Name the old boxes that are presently on the table. Empty an old box onto the table, spilling out fresh and old boxes along the way. Then, place the empty box on the ground. Examine every trinket; if it's *Red*, your quest is over; if not, put it on the ground. Once you've used all the old boxes, start the process again, and that is a breadth-first search.

2.3.2 Depth-First Search

An algorithm called *Depth-First Search* (DFS) traverses each branch as far as it can before turning around. The idea behind DFS is to take a different route after going as far down a single path as possible until you accomplish a goal or can no longer go further. The *Last-In-First-Out* stack data structure can be used to achieve DFS. Every visited node is tracked using the stack. In addition, DFS is utilized for *Path-Finding*, *Topological Sorting*, *Graph Cycle Detection*, and *Bipartite Graph* testing [Nil82]. Let's examine an example of DFS working methods using the figure 2.1 we used to describe BFS. The root node, or the starting node, is initially inserted into the stack and designated as visited. After that, the top of the stack is examined, and the next unvisited node is pushed into the stack in alphabetical order. Recall that one node at a time is pushed into the stack. A top-of-stack node is popped out of the stack if it has no unvisited nodes. Proceed again after that, keeping an eye on the top nodes until the stack is empty. We have to halt every process if the stack becomes empty. Eventually, the output sequence is produced, which includes ABSCDEHGF and others. Time and space complexity, completeness, and optimality were used to assess this algorithm's performance. Considering the first completeness, DFS is complete as it provides the solution. Only when every node has the exact path cost can DFS produce an optimal result for the optimality parameter. Regarding time and space complexity, the time and memory requirements rise in tandem with the search tree's level or the tree's depth. Therefore, this DFS algorithm has an $\mathcal{O}(b^d)$ time complexity and $\mathcal{O}(bd)$ space complexity, where b is the number of nodes and d is the number of levels in the search tree of a graph. Let us take the same example we covered in the previous section 2.3.1. Alternatively, you could *Stack* every box on the table's left side. The next step is to take a box from the farthest pile on the right and empty its contents onto a new pile to the right of the previous pile, with the empty box falling to the ground. Then, go through each object until a red one is located, discarding the others. It is a depth-first search. Let's look at a straightforward real-time example for ease of understanding. Suppose you have a map, or rather, a graph of cities. After beginning in a city, you travel to one of its neighboring ones. While in the adjacent city, you visit one of its neighboring cities. You have marked cities on your checklist to avoid visiting the same place twice. Eventually, you'll come to a city without more travel options because your neighboring cities have already traveled. So you circle back on your original path until you come upon a city that has not been visited and follow that path. You visit every city on this graph until it is all filled in, or if you have a goal, you can attain it by traveling to every city whose name begins with the letter 'A' until reached. We refer to this kind of depth-searching method as a depth-first search.

2.3.3   Bidirectional Search

A bidirectional search is an uninformed strategy that conducts two searches simultaneously. There are two types of search: *Backward Search*, which begins at the goal state, and *Forward Search*, which starts from an initial state. When these two searches get to an intersection, they both stop. Various search algorithms, including *BFS* and *DFS*, can be used in *Bidirectional Search*. It is essential to remember that the BFS method used in the beginning state is also used in the goal state; similarly, comparable algorithms must be used on both sides [Nil82]. For instance, the BFS algorithm is used on both sides in figure 2.2, and ultimately, the two searches cross at node 7, representing the optimal solution. The bidirectional algorithm finds the *Shortest Path* between the initial and goal states on a directed graph. It is a quicker method that decreases the time needed for *Graph Traversal.* It is also efficient when the starting and goal states are distinct and well-defined. Furthermore, for both directions, the branching

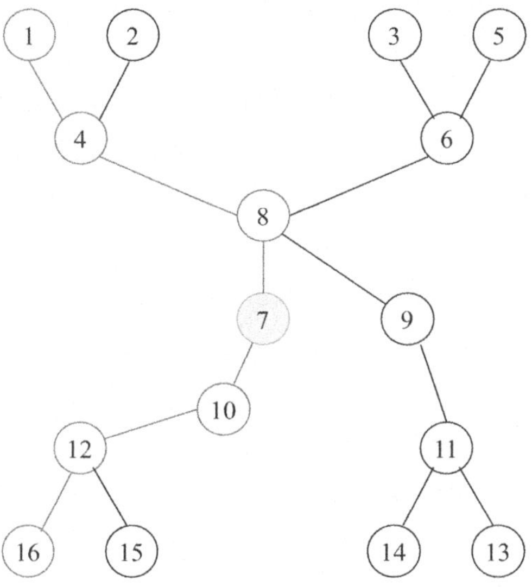

Figure 2.2: The General Example of Bidirectional Search

factors are the same. The performance of this algorithm was assessed in terms of *Optimality,* time and space complexity, and completeness. If we utilize BFS on both sides and the branching factor is finite, then the bidirectional search is complete. When bidirectionality is used correctly, it yields excellent solutions, like node 7. If BFS search is employed, the bidirectional algorithm's time and complexity are $\mathcal{O}(b^{d/2})$, where d is the search tree's depth and b is the branching factor. Because of its excellent efficiency, this technique is applied in many real-world scenarios, such as robots and *Computer Game Pathfinding*. When a game has a big map, the algorithm can determine the best route for a character while considering topography and barriers. Regarding *Robotics*, the algorithm determines the best path a robot can take while moving from one place to another, considering any potential impediments in its surroundings. Let's look at the second illustration: *GPS Navigation Systems* frequently employ bidirectional search to determine the quickest route between the origin and destination locations. From the beginning location to the destination, the algorithm searches outward until it comes to a meeting point in the middle to create the best possible path, which gives consumers a precise and quick route to their location while drastically reducing search time. Lastly, bidirectional search can determine the smallest distance, the number of connections between two people on *Social Networks* such as *Facebook* or

LinkedIn. The algorithm can swiftly determine the best route between people by exploring the source and target profiles simultaneously. This can help find relationships between individuals, recommend possible friends or colleagues, or support network analysis research.

2.3.4 Uniform-Cost Search

In a *Weighted Graph* where the cost of each edge is a positive number, the *Uniform-Cost Search* (UCS) search method determines the least expensive path from a start state to a goal state. When distinct costs are available for every step, this algorithm is employed. Because *UCS* does not rely on *Heuristics*, it is the *Optimal* algorithm for a search issue. It can find the best cost in various general graphs [Nil82]. As the name suggests, UCS offers branches with roughly equal costs. UCS requires the use of a *Priority Queue*. As you may remember, DFS employed a priority queue, where the element stored was the path from the root to the node, and the priority was the depth up to that node. Similar priority queues are employed here, where the node's cumulative cost determines the priority. In UCS, the most minor cost has the highest priority, whereas in DFS, the maximum depth has the highest priority. Let's see how the UCS algorithm operates. Place the root first in the queue. It is now necessary for us to verify if the queue is empty. *Dequeue* the element with the highest priority from the queue if the condition is met. An alphabetically smaller path is selected if the priorities are the same. If it ends in the *Goal State*, the process should be completed by printing the path. If not, insert every child of the dequeued element, giving the total costs precedence. Let's examine what happens when we apply the algorithm in Figure 2.4. We will look at the outcome after going through each cycle. Since node S is a root node, there are initially three options. We must select node T as the least expensive path among these options. Now that node T has two options, we must choose node R, which has the lowest path cost, out of the two options. Currently, two paths are available to node R; we must select the one with the lowest cost, node $G2$, which is the goal node. As a result, the procedure must be stopped. This path comes with a total cost of 13. Finding the *Shortest Path* can be done this way. At any given execution stage, the algorithm never expands a node whose cost exceeds the cost of the graph's shortest path. Uniform Cost Search gets its

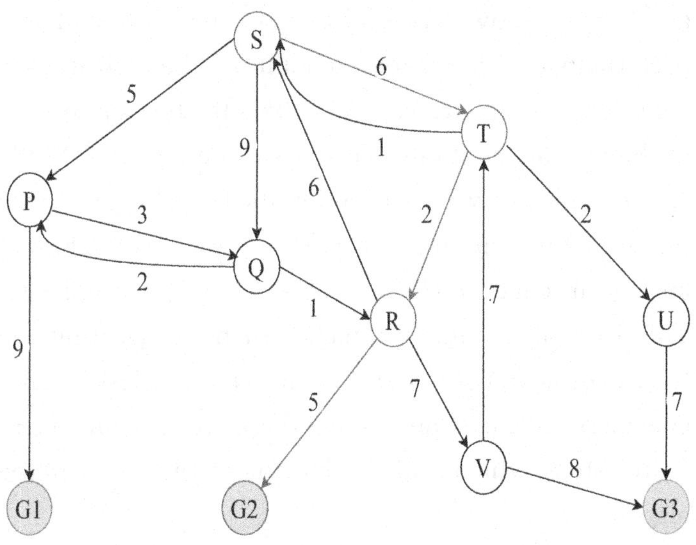

Figure 2.3: Typical Example of Uniform-Cost Search

name because the components in the priority queue at any given time have nearly identical costs. The pieces in the example above have very different costs. However, this is the case when applied to a much bigger graph. If the cost of each edge is set to 1, UCS can also function as a BFS. It is now necessary to assess the UCS method's performance; if it provides a solution, the algorithm is considered complete. The UCS offers the best option out of the available options. This algorithm has an $\mathcal{O}(b^{c/d})$ time complexity, where b denotes the branching factors,c represents the optimal solution cost, and e is the lowest cost of an edge. $\mathcal{O}(b^{c/e})$ is also the space complexity. This UCS algorithm's primary benefit is selecting the least expensive path at each state. Nevertheless, it only considers path cost and is indifferent to the number of search steps, which could lead to an indefinite loop in the algorithm.

2.4   Informed Search

Knowing the estimated distance between the present state and the goal state is one of the ways that an *Informed Search* differs from an *Uninformed Search*. It's sometimes called a guided or *Heuristic Search*. The *Heuristic Function* directs the node traversal by indicating how far each node is from the goal node. Let's use the same example from the previous chapter 2.3 to further comprehend the idea of an informed search. Assume that we know the *Password* is made up entirely of *Prime Numbers*. This type of domain knowledge is based on reliable information that we have obtained from various sources. Therefore, we can apply this knowledge to our problem-solving strategy as a heuristic. Just four prime numbers, 2, 3, 5, and 7, add up to nine. We don't need to look for as many combinations as in the earlier section 2.3. The number of alternatives in this case will be 4^8, which means that there are four possible values for each digit and a total of eight digits. There are only 65536 possible outcomes as a result. Approximately 99.4% fewer options or solutions were available. The number of potential answer percentages rises directly with the decrease in search digits. The term for this whole procedure is an informed search. Some basic, well-informed search algorithms are covered in the following sections.

2.4.1   Best-First Search

In contrast to uninformed search, which has the agent go unthinkingly to the next node, *Best-First Search* utilizes an *Evaluation Function* to determine which of the multiple accessible nodes is the most promising before traversing to that node. The Best-First Search uses the ideas of *Heuristic Search* and a *Priority Queue*. The Best-First Search approach tracks the traversal using two lists to search the graph space. A closed list records the nodes that have already been traversed, while an open list records the nodes that are currently immediately accessible for traversal. Let's now examine how the Best-First Search algorithm operates. Make an open and closed list as your first two blank lists. Add the original node to the sorted open list first. Proceed with the necessary steps until you arrive at the destination node. Get out of the loop and return a false statement stating that the last node cannot be reached if the open list is empty. Next, while maintaining an eye on the parent node, pick the top node in the open list and move it to the closed list. The goal node moves the node to the closed list and returns a true statement indicating that a path has been found if the node is removed. List all nearby nodes and add them to the open list if they are not the desired nodes. Reorder the nodes based on the evaluation function [Ert18]. To help you better comprehend, let's start with this Figure 2.4.

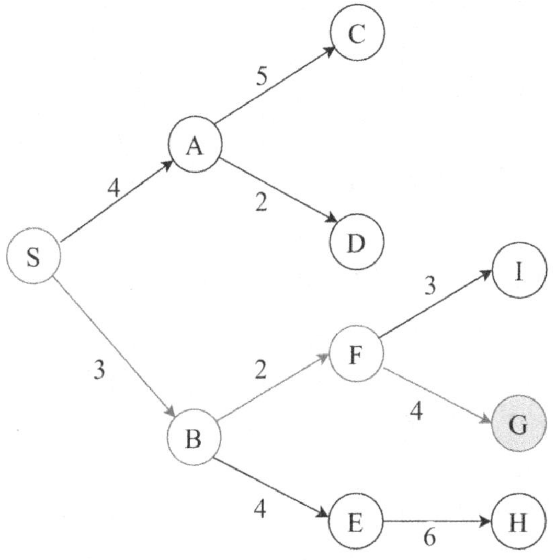

Figure 2.4: Standard Illustration of Best-First Search

The Table 2.1 contains the *Heuristic Value* corresponding to each node. Two lists—the open list and the closed list—are used. At first, node S is in the open list, and there is nothing in the closed list. In the initial iteration, we remove node S and add it to the closed list while adding the neighboring nodes to the open list. The heuristic

61

Table 2.1: Best-First Search: Heuristic Value Associated with Each Node

Node	A	B	C	D	E	F	H	I	S	G
Heuristic Value	12	4	7	3	8	2	4	9	13	0

values of nodes *A* and *B* are compared for the second iteration, and since *B* has a lower heuristic, it is picked and added to the closed list. *B*'s surrounding nodes are moved to the open list. The heuristic values of *E*, *F*, and *A* are compared for the third iteration, and since *F* has the lowest heuristic, it is included in the closed list. *F*'s neighbors are now included in the open list. Since our target node is already in the open list for the fourth iteration, we choose it and move it to the closed list. The route thus followed is S→B→F→G. Let's now assess this algorithm's performance. When n is the number of nodes, the worst-case time complexity of the best-first search is $\mathcal{O}(n \log n)$. In the worst situation, we must visit every node before finishing the task. Note that insert and remove operations take $\mathcal{O}(\log n)$ time, and the priority queue is implemented using *Min Heap* or *Max Heap*. The cost or evaluation function's design impacts the algorithm's performance.

2.4.2   Greedy Best First Search

As an informed search algorithm, *Greedy Best First Search* (GBFS) employs heuristics to steer the search in the most promising direction. By determining the optimum next node to explore based on an evaluation function, *GBFS* is frequently used to handle some challenging issues, including *Pathfinding* in games, *Routing*, *Scheduling*, and *Optimization* challenges. The *Evaluation Function* calculates a node's quality by considering various parameters, including the projected cost of reaching the target and its distance. Furthermore, since only the heuristic value is considered, the evaluation and the *Heuristic Functions* are strictly equivalent. This strategy is predicated on the likelihood of a speedy resolution. However, since a shorter path might exist, the answer from a GBFS might not be optimal. The main advantage of GBFS is that it can be substantially faster than other search methods for some problems, especially those with many potential answers. But for other issues, when the heuristic evaluation function is not appropriate, GBFS may also be less valuable. It can take GBFS a while to figure out a solution [Heu19]. Let's examine the GBFS algorithm's operation. The GBFS method generates two empty lists, such as an open list and a closed list, much like the *Best-First Search*. Create a tree from scratch, using the root node as the open list's start node. Give back an incorrect assertion if the open node is empty. If not, append the current node to the list of closed nodes. Next, eliminate the node with the lowest heuristic value from the open list for exploration. Return a true statement if a child node is the target node. Otherwise, add the node to the open list for investigation if it hasn't already been on the closed or open lists. To enhance comprehension of GBFS, let us examine a basic example. Look at the accompanying Figure 2.5 and determine the route from A to G. In this instance, the heuristic values are rigorously used to measure the cost, shown in Table 2.2. In other words, how close it is to the goal. We first create

Table 2.2: GBFS: Heuristic Value Associated with Each Node

Node	A	B	C	D	E	F	H	I	S	G
Heuristic Value	10	9	8	6	9	4	6	3	11	0

two blank lists, an open and a closed list. The nearby nodes are added to the open list in the first iteration, and node *A* is removed and added to the closed list. In

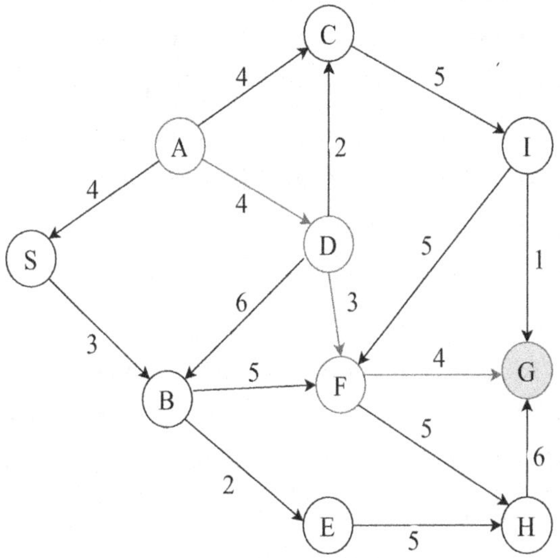

Figure 2.5:   General Illustration of Greedy Best-First
Search

the second iteration, D has the lowest cost—6—when compared to C and D. Thus, the search will continue in this manner. Since F had the lowest cost in the third iteration compared to B and C, F will be the next area of investigation. Ultimately, as G is the goal node, it has a heuristic value of 0. The path A→D→F→G has a total cost of 11. The path A→C→I→G has a cost of 10, which is less than A→D→F→G, indicating a possible issue with a GBFS. Because GBFS ignores edge weights, it disregarded this approach. It is now necessary to assess the GBFS algorithm's performance. This algorithm often combines *BFS* and *DFS*. Even though the state space is finite, GBFS is an incomplete set according to the first criterion. The second criterion states that the GBFS algorithm is not optimal. The worst-case time and space complexity of the GBFS are, respectively, $\mathcal{O}(b^m)$ and $\mathcal{O}(b^m)$, and m represents the maximum depth of the search space. Except for time and space complexity, the *A* Algorithm* solves completeness and optimality issues; this algorithm is covered in the following subsection 2.4.3.

2.4.3 A* Search

The *A* Search* algorithm is a knowledge-based search algorithm that employs a path-searching methodology. In 1968, Peter Hart, Nils Nilsson, and Bertram Raphael made the initial proposal [HNR68]. Heuristics are added to the method as an extension of *Dijkstra's Algorithm* to improve search efficiency. In order to determine the best route from the start node to the goal node, the iterative algorithm explores a graph's edges and assesses their costs. The three parameters of the A* algorithm are typically $g(n)$, $h(n)$, and $f(n)$. The actual traversal cost from the starting node to the current node is represented by $g(n)$. $H(n)$ represents the traversal cost from the current node to the goal node, and $f(n)$ represents the traversal cost from the beginning node to the goal node [LV12]. The A* algorithm operates by keeping track of visited nodes in two lists: open and closed. The method will choose the node from the open list with the lowest cost on each iteration, assess its neighbors, and add those nodes to the closed or open list. It will keep doing this until it gets to the objective node, at which time it will go back and find the quickest way by following its original path. Let's look at this algorithm's straightforward example for a better understanding. S is the start node, and G is the destination node, as seen in Figure 2.6. Since S is the starting node, the path traversal starts at S. Every node in Table 2.3 is assigned a specific set of

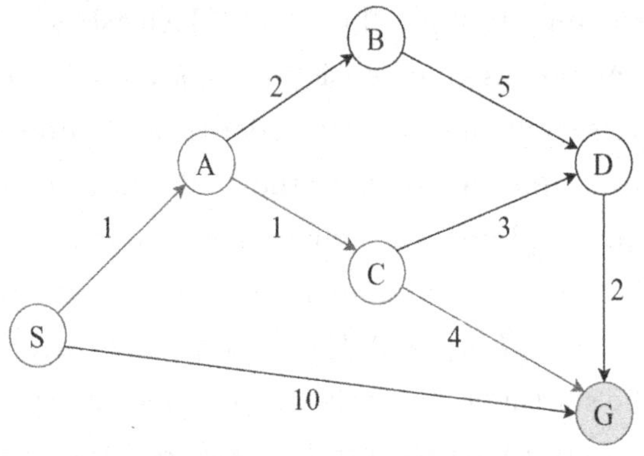

Figure 2.6: General Example of the A* Search Algorithm

Table 2.3: A* Search: Heuristic Value Associated with Each Node

Node or State	S	A	B	C	D	G
Heuristic Value	5	3	4	2	6	0

heuristic values. As previously stated, heuristic values represent the projected path cost to the objective node. We have considered the heuristic values in this instance, but we have done so with an eye toward practicality. Heuristic values determined using the formulas must be assigned to the A^* search. These formulas may include the node search formula, the *Manhattan Distance* formula for graphs, and the *Euclidean Distance* formula. They may also differ depending on how the method is used. The formula $f(n)=g(n)+h(n)$ is used to compute the path cost of the nodes that are near S. In this case, The nodes next to S are A and G. Only the shortest path is considered. In this instance, S→A is the shortest path and holds the S→G path. Next, a new search is conducted for the nearby nodes. B and C are adjacent nodes to A. Once more, repeat the process. S→A→C is the smallest path, containing S→A→B. The nearby nodes are now being searched for once more. D and G are adjacent nodes to C. Calculate the total cost next. As a result, S→A→C→G is the shortest path. The shortest path is found to be six from S→G, and the path is S→A→C→G because all the nodes have been checked, and the path has been calculated. We now need to assess this algorithm's performance. As long as the cost at each step is fixed and the branching factor is limited, the A^* algorithm is complete. Additionally, if the A^* algorithm satisfies two requirements, like acceptable, which indicates If there is a solution for the given problem, A* will first find an *Optimal* solution and then a consistent solution. This algorithm's time and space complexity is $\mathscr{O}(b^d)$ where d is the maximum depth of the search tree. The primary drawback of A* search is its *Memory Demand*, as it retains all the created nodes in memory, making it impractical for various large-scale issues.

2.5   Local Search in Discrete Environments

Both uninformed and informed search techniques systematically operate and identify solutions as necessary. On the other hand, *Local Search* is entirely different in looking for the best solution for each movement. This is why it offers a multitude of ideal solutions. The local state space search environment has limited *Perceptions* and *Actions*. They are stated differently in a *Discrete Environment*. Typically, *Greedy Search* approaches are applied to local search algorithms to tackle regional *Optimization* issues. Local search uses investigation and assessment to find the optimal result. To achieve this, it will assess several solutions using *Heuristics* and other techniques until it locates one that satisfies the user's specific requirements. This could involve figuring out the cheapest choice for a particular item or the most effective path between two locations. Put another perspective: local search can be compared to a climber ascending a mountain; they would make tiny adjustments to their course and always aim for the peak. It usually finds a near-optimal solution and focuses on obtaining a decent answer by making little changes to an existing solution. Furthermore, users can construct their apps based on the parameters they provide by using a local search *Application Programming Interface* or *API* available with software packages such as *Wolfram Alpha*. Local search has grown in popularity because it can rapidly get the best answers from massive datasets with minimal user involvement. It can be used for more complicated problem-solving situations when several factors must be assessed over extended or limited time beyond simple mapping assignments. Because of this, it offers developers and engineers a practical means of optimizing systems while lowering risk exposure while working with ambiguous *Data Sets*. The main issue with this kind of search is *Local Optima*, or, in other words, whatever works best for a single component's performance. Local search is essential to power *Decision-Support Systems* and produces precise *Recommendations.* In the following subsections, look at a few local search algorithms for solving *Complex Problems* in discrete environments.

2.5.1   Hill Climbing Search

The *Hill Climbing Algorithm* is a locally optimized search technique that iteratively advances toward the *Optimal Solution* or the top of the mountain. When it hits a peak value, and no neighbor has a higher value, it ends. It's a method for making mathematical problems more optimal. A well-cited example of a hill climbing algorithm is the *Traveling Salesman Problem*, which aims to minimize the salesman's journey distance. It is also known as a *Greedy Local Search* because it just seeks its good immediate neighbor state and not elsewhere. The two parts of a node in a hill climbing algorithm are value and state. When a reliable heuristic is accessible, it is primarily utilized. Since this algorithm stores one current state, we don't need to manage or maintain the search tree or graph. While the greedy approach to search proceeds in the direction that minimizes the cost, hill climbing is typically a variation of the generate and test method that produces feedback that helps to decide which way to move in the search space. Furthermore, because it cannot remember past states, it does not retrace the search space. The search's overall objective is to locate the local and *Global Maximums* [SG06]. Let's now examine how the hill-climbing algorithm operates. First, assess the starting point as it is at this moment. If that is the desired state, go back and end the process. If not, repeat the cycle until a solution is discovered or no more processes are available for comparison. Choose a new state for comparison afterward, and then assess the new state. We have three options for determining the new state. First, stop the procedure if it is in the desired state, like reaching the most significant peak. Make it the new current state if it is superior to the present one. If it turns out not to be better than the situation as it is, the cycle is repeated until a solution is found. Let's look at a straightforward real-time scenario to help you better comprehend hill climbing. Let's say you have a goal that you would like to achieve maximum success in, like generating the most *Revenue*, removing *Wheat*, or removing *Carbon* from the atmosphere. Imagine the quantity as the height or altitude you wish to maximize. Thus, one foot of altitude equals 100,000 rupees, 10,000 bushels of wheat, or one ton of carbon removed. Your strategy is represented by where you are on the map. Assume you spend 30% on utilities, 30% on travel, and 40% on medical care. The three numbers, 30, 30, and 40, indicate your position. Let's say you choose to shift 2% from utilities to transportation. That is a shift in your posture that will either move you down the slope or higher up. An objective and a model that forecasts the impact of the change are required. You search for another move from your current position after making one. You carry on from there each time you discover a wise move. The goal is to ascend to the top gradually. While processing the hill climbing algorithm, a few issues come up. The first significant issue is a *Local Maximum*, which denotes a state superior to every other state that borders it but is not at the top of the hill. Furthermore, since a *Plateau* is a flat region, it cannot be superior to the current point in the search space since no neighboring state exists because they are all on the same plane. Lastly, a search space region is elevated above its surroundings but could be more practical to search across with a single motion. As a result, we must use an alternative process, such as simulated annealing, which is discussed in the following section 2.5.2.

2.5.2   Simulated Annealing Search

Heuristic algorithms such as *Simulated Annealing* are frequently employed to resolve discrete global optimization issues, such as the *Traveling Salesman Problem*. Hill climbing encounters difficulties when it reaches a local optimum; they are resolved via simulated annealing. Let's begin by discussing the fundamental concept that underlies the algorithm's name. Simulated annealing can assist you in finding the minimum by allowing you to go from one branch to another while optimizing one at a time. We will eventually be able to understand the analogy if we begin with the concept that underlies the algorithm's name. Let's take an example where a metal is heated to a suitable *Temperature*, and we only need to cool it down. This cooling process can now be carried out either carefully, gradually, or quickly. *Crystallization* occurs when cooling occurs, and rushing the process produces smaller-sized metal crystals that form an extremely brittle metal framework. On the other hand, a progressive approach enables the crystals to form larger, more robust crystals, which makes the cooled metal structure relatively stable. This cooling process, which happens gradually, is called annealing [Van+87]. We transferred job after job and city after city in our early years because we were very energetic. Without anticipating imminent gain, energy is needed to overcome an immediate obstacle. As we age, we settle into a scenario that will last the rest of our lives. We adhere to the simulated annealing. Temperature is the most significant parameter in simulated annealing compared to natural energy. The threshold at which something can be crossed without instant benefit is determined by temperature. Let's now examine how the simulated annealing process operates. In the whole search space, the algorithm looks for the peak point. It searches the area around its current position for higher places, but now and then, it will move with a probability to a lower point, which aids in escaping the local maximum problem. Now, the temperature is kept high to increase the likelihood that comparably worse solutions will be accepted in the beginning compared to the existing solution, with the primary goal being to emphasize exploration.

In order to make the algorithm finally converge to a solution that is, if not precisely the global maximum, then at least extremely close to it, the points in the vicinity of the current solution are searched recursively, and the temperature parameter is gradually reduced. That's all there is to annealing simulation. To put it another way, add a *Temperature Parameter* to the loop. Next, make a random new move and assess whether you won or lost in the altered circumstances. If there is a gain, proceed; if there is a loss, check the temperature; if it is high enough to offset the loss, move; if not, stay put. If the temperature is zero, break out of the loop, lower the temperature, and repeat the process until the *Global Optimization* is reached. Let's examine a few real-world situations to gain a better idea. Assume **X**, an 18-year-old male, faces the challenge of locating the ideal *Laptop*. **X** approaches the problem in two different ways. He has two options: he can prioritize exploitation or, more technically, explore more, meaning he will keep searching until he finds the ideal laptop, or he may wish to settle on the first one he likes. As one might expect, neither of these methods will work properly. You might finally find the perfect laptop with the existing one. Even so, it could be better when you eventually get a laptop because you might be approaching your 60s. Conversely, the latter lets you work hard for several months or even a year before the inevitable damage happens. Therefore, the best strategy for choosing a laptop would be to start with a more extensive set of exploratory criteria and concentrate more on exploitation once you have selected a laptop—one that may not be perfect, but it should be decent enough. In essence, this is what simulated annealing accomplishes. The cooling schedule requires careful setup, which is the main issue with the simulated annealing search process. An algorithm may converge to a local optimum if it is run too quickly, or it may take too long to connect if it is run too slowly. Furthermore, finding a decent solution may take a lot of iteration, particularly in complex situations. The genetic algorithm search, covered in the following section 2.5.3, solves these issues.

2.5.3   Genetic Algorithm Search

Search using *Genetic Algorithms* (GA) is an effective method for solving optimization issues. For every member of a *Population*, the GA employs binary-coded solutions—such as *DeoxyriboNucleic Acid* or *DNA*—for the optimization problem [Bro11]. Three main processes lead to the evolution of such a population: *Mutation, Crossover,* and *Selection.* A set of matched parents is selected randomly for each iteration, meaning multiple random techniques are available to choose these parent pairings. Next, the selection process considers the fitness value of choosing responsible parents. Under the theory that two well-adapted parents have a high probability of producing more adapted children, the crossover is performed over each pair of chosen parents, in which their DNA is mingled to generate two new solutions that mean offspring. The first step in mixing the chromosomes is to divide them into four sections by randomly choosing a portion of the string to serve as a pivot. Then, combining the opposing parts results in two new solutions. Some alternative algorithms perform the chain split using multiple pivots. Every freshly created solution subsequently has a negligible probability of experiencing random mutations on one or more binary string segments of their *Chromosome.* Rather than directing the search straight toward well-known *Local*

Optima, this helps the search to comb over the search space [ČLM13]. In the end, the population is made up

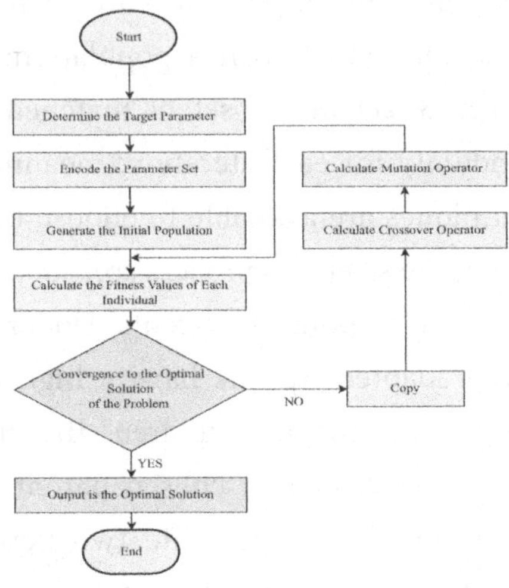

Figure 2.7: Flowchart of the Genetic Algorithm Search

of more solutions. As resources are scarce in the natural world, only the most adaptable individuals survive, aligning with the species *Evolution Theory*. The most well-known options are chosen through a final selection procedure to continue in the following iterations, while the others are eliminated. The Figure 2.7 depicts the general genetic algorithm flow. Despite the *Greedy* technique used in Holland's initial method [Hol92], the selection strategy is crucial to balancing *Exploration* and *Exploitation.* These are the genetic algorithm's fundamental features. But before using this approach to solve an optimization problem, you must create the heuristic code, decode the binary strings representing the answers, and suggest a fitness function that assigns a dependable numerical score to each solution. To increase the lift-to-drag ratio for a complicated wing, let's examine one application of GA to an aviation wing design problem. When faced with multidisciplinary issues such as these, the fitness functions of the GA can be tailored to meet the unique needs of the current design. In competitive product development circumstances, this is frequently necessary. Another use is a failed research trial to identify patient subgroups that could benefit from the medication. A genetic algorithm determines the optimal subset of entrance requirements regarding likely sample size and drug reaction. Finally, based solely on that patient subset, the simulation and revised criteria indicate a high likelihood of trial success. Financial time series analysis is also using GAs more and more. Analogous techniques, such as ant colony and *Particle Swarm Optimization*, which we discuss in the next section

2.5.4, are also becoming more popular. GA could be more efficient when used in its most basic version. This is primarily because they have a restricted search space due to design choices regarding the chromosome structure, regularly recalculate fitness functions, and are prone to convergence. One needs to be conscious of the appearance of the data when using them. Experience is the only thing that can provide this. Nonetheless, their high degree of parallelism makes them advantageous to use. *Fitness Evaluation* is the most computationally demanding learning process. This stage operates independently of each member of the population. This implies that, in a population of one million, each person might be assigned to a different computer, and each laptop could assess fitness independently of the others. Other approaches are more difficult to use, so their popularity persists despite these drawbacks. GA algorithms have existed for over 60 years and are still the first choice for engineering and optimization tasks where computational speed isn't a significant concern. Global optimization algorithms offer solutions to problems that are difficult to solve using existing optimization techniques. These days, *Quantum-Inspired*

Genetic Algorithms (QIGA) and other new extensions and improvements of genetic algorithms are becoming more popular, and we anticipate that further research and development will be done to enhance further compute times and accuracy. Research on *QIGA* is fascinating, as it may be able to address some of the drawbacks associated with genetic algorithms. In summary, genetic algorithms and their more distant cousins, such as QIGA, will be big things in optimization in the future.

2.5.4   Artificial Ant Colony Search

The *Artificial Ant Colony Search*, or *AACS* technique, is a *Metaheuristic* approach to challenging optimization issues. Ants' ability to determine the shortest route between their colony and a food source serves as the model for AACS. An algorithm known as AACS builds solutions to a problem piecemeal, just like ants do. Through a succession of site selections, each ant constructs its own solution. The ultimate answer is created by combining the solutions each ant developed. In 1992, Marco Dorigo presented *Ant Colony Search* or *ACS* for the first time in his doctoral thesis [Dor92]. It was first applied to solve the well-known traveling salesman problem. Subsequently, it was employed to resolve several challenging optimization issues. Social insects are ants. Colonies are where they reside. The ants' primary objective in their food search is to find food. An ant is regarded as an *Artificial Ant Agent* in AI. Artificial ants are prowling throughout the colonies in quest of food. An artificial ant keeps hopping from one location to another to locate food. When it moves, it leaves an organic substance known as *Pheromone* on the ground. Artificial ants use pheromone trails to communicate with one another. An artificial ant brings as much food as possible when it comes across some. Upon its return, it places pheromones on the pathways according to the amount and caliber of food. An artificial ant has pheromone sense. Other artificial ants will, therefore, be able to smell it and follow the trail. The likelihood of selecting that road increases with pheromone level, and the more artificial ants that follow the path, the more pheromone there is on that trail. Let us examine the two possible routes to obtain food from the colony. There isn't any pheromone on the ground initially. Therefore, there is an equal chance of picking either of these two pathways or 50%. Assume that two artificial ants have a fifty-

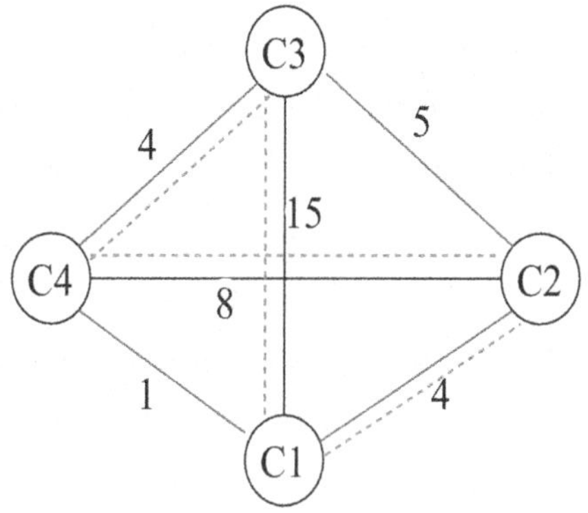

Figure 2.8: AACS: Cost and Distance of a Graph

Table 2.4: AACS: Cost and Distance of Travelling Salesman Problem

Cities	C1	C2	C3	C4
C1	0	4	15	1
C2	4	0	5	8
C3	15	5	0	4
C4	1	8	4	0

fifty chance of selecting two distinct routes to get to the meal. These two pathways have different distances. The artificial ant that takes the shortest route will get to the meal before the others. It returns to the colony with some food that it found and carries with it. It leaves pheromone deposits on the ground as it tracks back. The artificial ant that takes the quicker route will arrive at the colony sooner. Based on the pheromone level on the ground, the third artificial ant will choose the path with the shortest distance when it decides to venture outside in search of food. The third artificial ant will follow the trail with more pheromones because it is shorter than the longer one. More artificial ants had already followed the path with higher pheromone levels by the time the artificial ant that had taken the longer route returned to the colony. Upon reaching the target, which is the colony's food supply, another artificial ant will discover that every trail has the same pheromone level. It selects one at random, then.

After repeatedly going through this procedure, the shorter trail eventually has a higher pheromone level than the others and is more likely to be followed; as a result, all artificial ants will choose the shorter way the next time. Put another way, an artificial ant is designed to locate the best answer. Every ant provides a solution as the initial step in issue-solving. The trails that various ants found are compared in the second stage. The third stage involves updating the pheromone or pathway value. AACS can be used to identify the best answer for various optimization problems, including *Timetable Scheduling, Train Scheduling, Traveling Salesman Problem,* and more. Look at real-world AACS algorithm examples, like *TSP.* Using the cost and distance matrix in Table 2.4 and Figure 2.8, assume there are four cities, C1, C2, C3, and C4, and that salespeople S1 and S2 wish to travel across all the cities in the best possible way. Two possible routes, such as R1 and R2, are available. The colors blue and red denote R1 and R2, respectively. There is a 50% chance that R1 and R2 will select the best solution. For instance, S1→R1 has a total distance cost of 14 while S2→R2 has a total distance cost of 31. The best solution approach, S1→R1, is the minimum cost route, so we must choose it while comparing these options. This is how the AACS method was used to find the shortest path. Given that the fundamental AACS algorithm has poor early-stage convergence speed and blind search, *Tabu Search* is looking for a solution, which we discussed in the following section 2.5.5.

2.5.5 Tabu Search

Another popular *Metaheuristic* method for handling discrete optimization issues is *Tabu Search*, which *Fred Glover* developed in the late 1980s [Glo89]. To save time, it keeps track of recently investigated solutions in *Short-Term Memory*, or *Tabu-List*, which keeps the search too narrow and keeps the algorithm from becoming stuck in *Local Optima*. *Intensification* techniques are employed in tabu search to investigate potential regions inside the solution space. It can be seen as a more comprehensive version of the *Simulated Annealing* algorithm covered in this section 2.5.2. Numerous issues, including *Scheduling*, *Supply Chain Optimization*, and *Resource Allocation*, can be resolved using the tabu search algorithm. The two main memory structure types tabu searches use are short-term and *Long-Term Memory*. There are typically a limited number of previously explored options stored in short-term memory that we shouldn't revisit. This will aid in expanding the search while it's in long-term

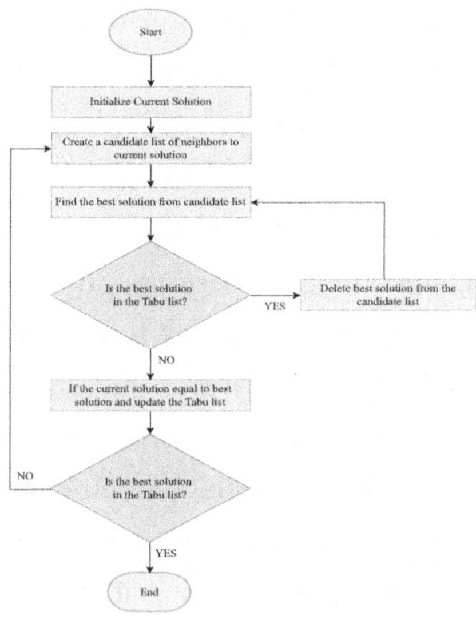

Figure 2.9: Flowchart of the Tabu Search Algorithm

memory and assist when the search gets stuck. Having one, the other, or even both, is optional. The fundamental concept is to monitor the algorithm's actions and assist it in exploring various potential solutions. Let's examine the tabu search algorithm's operational mechanisms. First, come up with a working solution. Next, a local search will be used to obtain a set of potential neighborhood solutions from the existing solution. Find the best candidate not on the tabu-list from these neighborhood solutions. Subsequently, evaluate this top contender against the best existing option and designate accordingly. The value of the top candidate should then be added to the tabu-list. Once more, carry out the procedure with the top contender to create the new community until specific requirements are met. Additional criteria, known as the ambition criterion, state that we accept a solution even if it is on the tabu list and has a more significant objective function than the best solution available at the time. This is how the best solution is found using the tabu search method. Figure 2.9 depicts the tabu search algorithm's general workflow. This approach produced excellent outcomes when used to solve the *Traveling Salesman Problem,* which we discussed in the previous section 2.5.4 as an example.

2.6 Constraint Satisfaction Problem

Artificial intelligence aims to build intelligent machines capable of carrying out tasks that call for *Human Intelligence*. Solving problems is a crucial component of *AI*, and a standard paradigm for solving problems in AI is the *Constraint Satisfaction Problem* or *CSP*. In artificial intelligence, CSP is a famous computational problem with clear definitions. CSP is a collection of mathematically stated questions that must adhere to numerical restrictions. Put another way, and it's the process of figuring out how to get around a set of restrictions that present requirements that the variables must meet. It depicts an issue as a set of limitations that must be overcome using CSP techniques. A condition or rule that restricts the range of potential solutions to a problem is referred to as a constraint in the definition of a constraint satisfaction problem. These limitations can be subtle, like preferences or limitations, or explicit, like *Logical Rules* or mathematical calculations. A CSP aims to find a solution that complies with every constraint. Numerous real-world issues, including *Scheduling*, *Planning*, *Resource Allocation*, and *Puzzles*, can be modeled using CSPs. Specifying variables, domains, and constraints offers a formal and structured method for representing and resolving complicated issues. The variables in a CSP stand for the problem's unknowns, while the domains specify the range of values that each variable is capable of. The constraints, which restrict their possible values, describe the connections or dependencies between the variables. AI algorithms utilize various strategies to solve CSPs, including *Constraint Propagation*, *Local Search*, and *Backtracking*. By considering the limitations and making well-informed decisions to direct the search toward a workable solution, these strategies examine potential solutions' search space methodically. To enhance comprehension, let's see a simple real-world CSP example. We are aware that there are limitations on everything. The limitations of the universe that we study in *Physics* impose restrictions on our brains. Everything is dependent on how tight those restrictions are. Let's look at some detailed directions for making tea. Alternatively, we might advise you to try preparing tea—do anything you can in the kitchen as long as the result is a tea that you will drink. The second scenario allows you to be creative, learn, and explore more than the first one, which offers less room for improvisation. The same idea holds for developing and teaching AI: the more flexible the environment, the more opportunities AI has to demonstrate its intelligence by being abstract and generic within the limits and end goals. The number of possible value combinations can increase exponentially with the number of variables and the size of their domains, making it difficult to solve a CSP efficiently. However, clever *Search Algorithms* and *Heuristics* can find complex CSP solutions in a reasonable amount of time. The following sections 2.6.1, 2.6.2, and 2.6.3 discuss the forms of CSP.

2.6.1   Traveling Salesman Problem

The *Traveling Salesman Problem*, or *TSP*, is a well-known challenging problem in AI optimization. Imagine a salesperson whose job is to visit a certain number of cities to sell their product. The objective is to determine the shortest path, enabling the salesman to travel to each city exactly once before returning to the starting place. The salesperson should minimize the money spent on travel and the distance covered. TSP, which focuses on optimization, is frequently used in computer science to determine the best path for transferring data between nodes. One use case is figuring out hardware or network optimization techniques. In the 1800s, Irish mathematician W.R. Hamilton and British mathematician Thomas Kirkman initially characterized it by devising a game that could be solved by identifying a *Hamilton Cycle* or a non-overlapping path connecting every node. A thorough analysis of Hamilton and Kirkman's work is found in the *Graph Theory* book [Big93]. Many theories have been proposed throughout the decades that TSP has been investigated. Trying every option is the easiest way to find a solution, but it is also the most costly and time-consuming. *Heuristics*, which produce probabilistic outcomes, are used in many solutions. The outcomes are not always ideal and are only approximations. *Las Vegas Algorithms* and *Branch-and-Bound Monte Carlo* are two other methods. TSP frequently prioritizes finding the least expensive solution over choosing the best action. Finding the shortest path in TSPs is difficult due to the many variables, which increases the appeal of approximate, quick, and affordable solutions. Let's discuss it with a simple example. The working

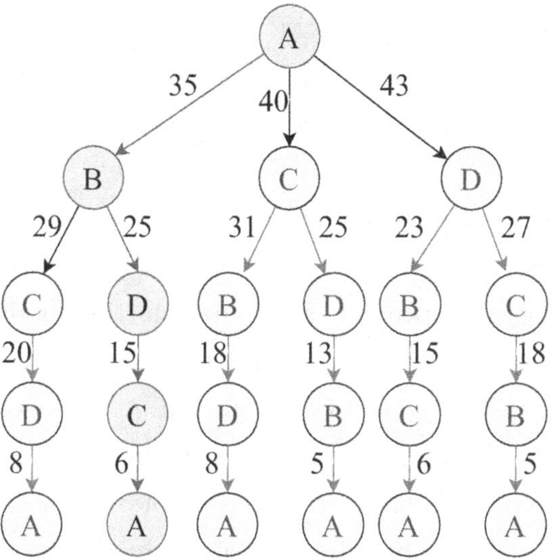

Figure 2.10: Typical TSP Operating Procedures with Dynamic Programming

process of the TSP algorithm is shown in Figure 2.10 and is connected to the cost matrix shown in Table 2.5. You may compute the cost from the base of this tree structure. Initially, the nodes with the lowest prices are D, C, D, B, C, and B. The cost values are then added to the node cost values from earlier. After the

Table 2.5: Cost of TSP Using Dynamic Programming

Cities	A	B	C	D
A	0	10	15	20
B	5	0	9	10
C	6	13	0	12
D	8	8	9	0

addition procedure, we must compare the cost values and select the node with the lowest cost value. Similarly, we must act until we reach the starting node. The Figure 2.10 shows six possible routes: A→B→C→D→A, A→B→D→C→A, A→C→B→D→A, A→D→B→C→A, and A→D→C→B→A. $A→B→D→C→A$ is the least expensive path and the best option for a given problem. This is how the TSP algorithm, using dynamic programming, operates. Let's look at an example in real time. Think about a delivery service like *UPS* or *United Parcel Service*. UPS makes use of over 90,000 trucks. Every truck begins its workday at a depot, travels to various locations, and ends at the depot. Although I'm not sure, I estimate that n would be between 20 and 50 in size for a standard vehicle. UPS could calculate a cost matrix to move the truck between each pair of n stops. Next, given this matrix, UPS wants to figure out how to address the truck's traveling salesman issue so that its route has the lowest total cost. Using *Brute Force* to solve the traveling-salesman problem would not be practical, even if UPS could compute the $n \times n$ matrix for free. Let's say the truck only makes 20 stops, and UPS can process one million orders every second. After that, it would take 28 days to sample each of the 20 orders throughout the 20 stops. That applies to one of the more than 90,000 trucks. UPS could save a large amount of money even if it could only increase the efficiency of its routes by 1%. Despite its many applications, TSP is still a computationally challenging issue, and even with powerful computers, finding precise solutions for extensive inputs can take a while.

2.6.2   Graph Coloring Problem

A drawing made up of lines that connect numbers is called a graph. A graph's function is to display data that is too large or complex to be sufficiently explained in text in a limited space. *Graphs* facilitate the viewing of information. This is particularly true if there is a relationship between two or more groups of numbers. In everyday calculations, we need to know the fundamentals of using graphs. It is available for all students, regardless of ability level, and is not reserved for math prodigies. Utilizing structure is essential when conducting any analysis. A graph will be used to do this. Making a graph can help with budget planning as well. After six months, you will be able to see areas where you are struggling and those where you are succeeding. Graphs are valuable for accountants when communicating financial information to their clients. A graph can be beneficial when gathering data and keeping it all in one location. Everyday publications like the neighborhood newspaper and magazine stand use graphs. It's one of those abilities you can't live without. Regardless of your requirement or computation, a graph can assist you and simplify your life when utilized appropriately. The issues in artificial intelligence are expressed as graphs. Thus, graphs are essential to AI. *Graph Coloring* is a significant problem within the problem domain that has influenced the development of graph theory. In *Graph Theory*, the graph coloring problem is coloring a graph's vertices to minimize the number of colors utilized while guaranteeing that no two neighboring vertices have the same color. Finding a coloring that uses the fewest colors is the aim, and the challenge is figuring out how many colors are needed to color a graph. It is known that the graph coloring problem is *NP-Hard*, meaning that it is at least as challenging as the most difficult *Non-Deterministic Polynomial-Time* problems. This indicates that a polynomial-time method has not yet solved the problem, and it is doubtful that one will ever be developed. On the other hand, numerous approximation algorithms, including backtracking and brute force, can effectively address the problem for large instances. The simplest method for solving this problem is *Brute Force*, which involves creating every possible arrangement or combination of colors. On the other hand, the complexity is enormous and exponential. Several permutation computations were repeated, even though they weren't necessary. Consequently, the plan is to tackle the issue by going *Backtracking*. The idea behind this method is to color a vertex and then select a different color for any nearby vertex that needs coloring. Similarly, color each vertex that can be found while adhering to the limitations, stopping at the last vertex to be colored. In any instance, adjust the color if a

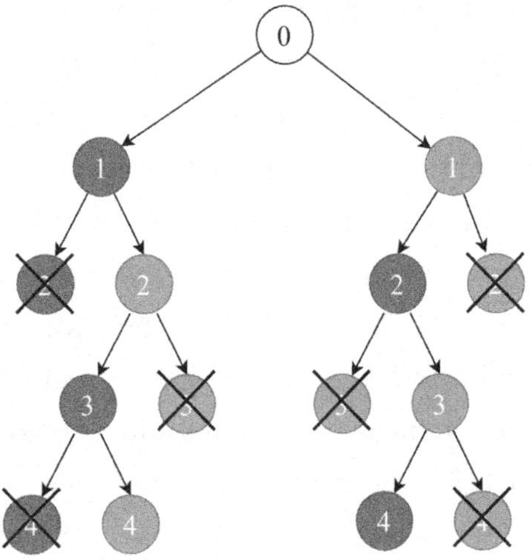

Figure 2.11: Graph Coloring Problem: General Working Methods with Backtracking

Vertex has colored nearby vertices. Additional colors are required if, after coloring, we go back to the original vertex and use every color. Thus, give back false. This algorithm operates in the following manner: Examine the validity of a color by determining whether or not its neighboring vertices have also been colored the same color, starting with the provided vertex. If this is the case, choose a different color; if not, keep coloring the vertices. Proceed back if no other color remains unused. This algorithm's worst-case time complexity is $\mathscr{O}(M^V)$, while its space complexity is $\mathscr{O}(V)$. M represents the colors of the graph, whereas V indicates vertices of the graph. The primary issue is that coloring vertices takes up additional space. Figure 2.11 provides a general instance of a graph coloring problem that was solved by backtracking. Let's now examine an example of a graph coloring problem. Problems with resource allocation are one setting in which graph coloring is used. The fundamental sequence is as follows: For any entity that requires a resource to be consumed from a pool of resources, create a node. Next, an edge between each pair of nodes will be added, requiring simultaneous resource usage. An interference graph is the name given to the resulting graph. Furthermore, ensure that no two nodes connected by an edge have the same color on the graph. The color now represents the resource allocated to the node-related entity. Everything in this sounds a little hazy, and that's intentional. Entities can represent various resource consumers, and colors can represent many interchangeable resources. *Graph Algorithms* are beautiful because they reduce issues to their most basic form. Graph coloring is mainly used in *Scheduling Problems* and *Register Allocation* in *Compilers*. Let's look at the example in real time to understand it better. Let's say you're attempting to place students in classrooms for a semester. Every class meets at a different hour and on a different day of the week. While some classes have time overlap, some don't. Reducing the overall number of rooms utilized is your goal. You can create the interference graph because you know the timetable in advance. Now, assign classes to rooms by coloring that graph. Try to determine a minimum coloration to reduce the number of rooms used. You have your homework for every class, and you can associate a color with each classroom. Graph coloring is a standard technique compilers use to map variables to *Processor*

Registers. Remember that not all register allocators use graph coloring, and even those that sometimes use extra techniques and heuristics besides graph coloring fundamentals. However, the core of many register allocators is the concept of graph coloring.

2.6.3 Sudoku Problem

In *Stuart Russell* and *Peter Norvig*'s words, AI is the process of making decisions in situations where it is unclear what is morally correct [RN16]. Many modern technologies, such as *Airline Reservation Systems* and *Google Maps Navigation*, were formerly considered artificial intelligence and would still fall under these criteria. This relates to the *Sudoku Problem* in that, to win, we must use inventive methods, including *Constraint Propagation* and iterative search algorithms. After completing all the apparent solutions in a round of the game, we have to guess the optimal course of action and then take it. By making that assumption more deliberate and systematic based on a plan, intelligence is put to use. Writing code that uses brute force to solve a problem given enough time and CPU power is relatively easy. The more intelligence we infuse into the system, the more intelligent it becomes. AI can use algorithms like *Backtracking* and *Brute Force* to sift through a large number of potential answers and select the one that is most likely to be accurate. An artificial intelligence system can utilize a method known as constraint satisfaction to solve a Sudoku problem. This method entails determining the constraints needed to discover a workable solution and then using this knowledge to focus the search for a solution. Additionally, the AI can explore potential solutions and select the one that best matches the puzzle's limitations using techniques like search and *Optimization* algorithms. There are three types of Sudoku puzzles: *Correctly Constrained, Under-Constrained,* and *Over-Constrained.* The over-constrained puzzle needs to be more solvable. A competent solver would be able to demonstrate that a particular puzzle is unsolvable. Puzzles with proper constraints only have one solution. A good solver would find this solution. Puzzles with too few constraints can have more than one solution. A competent solver could find at least one solution. It should be able to identify every potential solution if it doesn't give up on the first one. Well-constructed *Sudoku Puzzles* are in the middle. Any of the

	1				7	2	3	
2		5						4
3								
4				7				
				8				6
								7
5						3		8
	6	7	4				9	

(a) Partially Filled 9×9 2-Dimensional Array

6	1	8	9	4	7	2	3	5
2	7	5	1	6	3	9	8	4
3	9	4	5	2	8	6	7	1
4	3	6	2	7	5	8	1	9
7	8	2	6	1	9	4	5	3
1	5	9	3	8	4	7	2	6
9	2	3	8	5	6	1	4	7
5	4	1	7	9	2	3	6	8
8	6	7	4	3	1	5	9	2

(b) Fully Filled 9×9 2-Dimensional Array

Figure 2.12: Typical Example of a Sudoku Problem

three types of Sudoku-like puzzles should be manageable for a competent Sudoku solver. Look at a basic Sudoku solver that functions quickly on most machines. It only reports the first solution it discovers for puzzles that are not tightly limited. It's a straightforward *Recursive Algorithm*. First, locate the first square that is open in reading order. Then, submit a report if there are no open squares that mean success, print the answer, and be out of the loop. Once more, determine which digits remain viable choices for that place. Return failure and retrace one level if there are no valid digits. Furthermore, return failure and retrace one level if no valid numbers exist for that spot. If not, place each valid digit in the open square and continue recursively for each one. Go back to the failure and retrace your steps if they fail. The puzzle is solved if we go back to the beginning and still need to perceive success. That algorithm is efficient and reasonably straightforward. An illustration of a standard Sudoku puzzle is provided in Figure 2.12. The objective of the independent approach is to generate all possible configurations of numbers from 1 to 9 to fill the empty cells given a partially filled 9×9 2-dimensional array grid (9x9), as shown in Figure 2.12a. Try each configuration one at a time until the correct configuration is found. For example, fill each unassigned position with a number from 1 to 9. Check whether the matrix is safe after filling in all the unassigned positions. If safe, print; otherwise, it recurs for other cases. A filled 9×9 2-dimensional array is illustrated in Figure 2.12b. The time and space complexity of the Sudoku problem are $\mathcal{O}(9^{n*n})$ and $\mathcal{O}(n*n)$.

2.7 Summary

Agent-based state space search is a fundamental method for resolving intricate AI challenges. This chapter presents several general-purpose and problem-solving strategies. A discussion of uninformed search strategy algorithms follows an introduction to state space search. As a result of some issues being found, informed search strategy algorithms have been explored. Similar to this, some problems with informed search algorithms lead to the presentation of local search in a discrete context. Finally, several kinds of constraint satisfaction problems are discussed. The connection between the features of the problem and particular approaches ought to become even more apparent. Subsequently, the adversarial search strategies are covered in Chapter 3.

2.7.1 Multiple Choice Questions

Exercise 1: What is a problem-solving agent's primary work?

a) Solve the given problem and reach the goal state

b) To find out the longest path to reach a goal state

c) Problem-solving agents define the state of space

d) Problem-solving agents help to enhance the path cost

Exercise 2: What other term would one give to uninformed search strategies?

a) Guided search   b) Blind search

c) Unguided search   d) Sighted search

Exercise 3: What is the time complexity for a breadth-first search?

a) $\mathcal{O}(b^d)$ b) $\mathcal{O}(b^{c/d})$ c) $\mathcal{O}(bd)$ d) $\mathcal{O}(d^b)$

Exercise 4: What is the time complexity of Uniform-cost search?

a) $\mathcal{O}(b^{c/d})$ b) $\mathcal{O}(b^d)$ c) $\mathcal{O}(bd)$ d) $\mathcal{O}(b^c)$

Exercise 5: What is the time complexity of A* search?

a) $\mathscr{O}(b^{c/d})$ b) $\mathscr{O}(b^d)$ c) $\mathscr{O}(bd)$ d) $\mathscr{O}(b^c)$

Exercise 6: What other term would one give to informed search strategies?

a) Guided search b) Blind search

c) Unguided search d) Heuristic search

Exercise 7: Which search implements stack operation for searching the states?

a) Depth-limited search b) Depth-first search

c) Breadth-first search d) Bidirectional search

Exercise 8: Which search implements queue operation for searching the states?

a) Depth-limited search b) Depth-first search

c) Breadth-first search d) Uniform-cost search

Exercise 9: Which search approach requires the least memory?

a) Depth-limited search b) Depth-first search

c) Breadth-first search d) Bidirectional search

Exercise 10: Which is the heuristic function h(n)?

a) Lowest path cost

b) Cheapest path from the root to the goal node

c) Estimated cost of cheapest path from the root to the goal node

d) Average path cost

Exercise 11: Which is utilized to assist the generator in determining how far to travel in the search space?

a) Simulated annealing   b) Depth-first search

c) Breadth-first search   d) Hill climbing

Exercise 12: Which one is used to describe a similar simulated annealing process?

a) Diffusion annealing   b) Physical annealing

c) Isothermal annealing   d) Complete annealing

Exercise 13: What problem among the following can be a constraint satisfaction problem?

a) Graph coloring problem   b) Greedy best-first problem

c) Simulated annealing problem   d) Hill climbing problem

2.7.2   Short Answer Type Questions

1. Differentiate between depth-first and breadth-first searches.

2. Will the breadth-first search always yield the smallest solution? If yes, why?

3. Define heuristic search.   What advantages do heuristic searches offer?

4. How can performance in solving problems be assessed?

5. Why is goal formulation necessary after problem formulation?

6. What makes a person choose a heuristic search?

7. Give a reason why hill climbing frequently gets stuck.

8. In terms of search methodology, what do you mean by local maxima?

9. Define the CSP and enumerate its attributes.

2.7.3 Long Answer Type Questions

1. Perform the A* Algorithm on the figure 2.13:
   Explicitly write down the queue at each step.

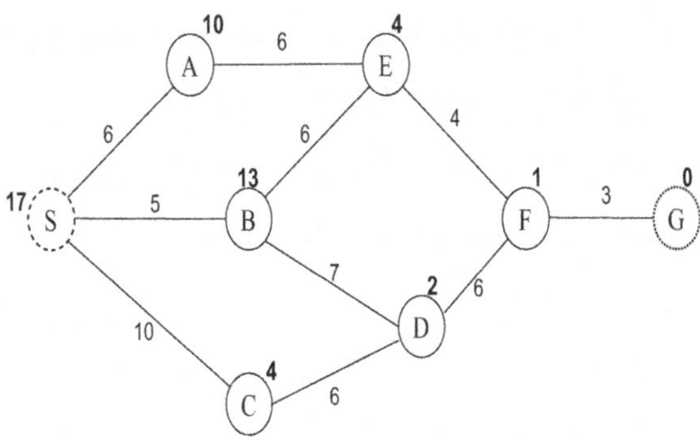

Figure 2.13: Question Figure for the A* Search Algorithm

2. Examine simulated annealing. Give an example of
   a real-world problem that uses simulated annealing
   to solve it.

3. Give an example to illustrate the nature of
   heuristics. What impact does the correctness of
   heuristics have?

4. Examine the constraint satisfaction problem using
   a Sudoku-solving algorithm.

Chapter 3

Adversarial Search to Find Best Moves

3.1   Goal of the Chapter

In the preceding chapter 2, single AI agents attempted to solve a given problem and reach a goal state through state space search. Two agents compete with one another during an adversarial search. This chapter, therefore, aims to determine the optimal course of action for a specific issue domain. Adversarial searching is concerned with making choices in situations with competition, such as those found in games and strategic engagements. An introduction and many adversarial search strategies are given in the ensuing sections.

3.2   Introduction

In an *Adversarial Search*, one agent attempts to plan ahead of time while other agents plan to hinder it. In *Multi-Agent* competitive situations, adversarial search challenges arise because an opponent beyond our control is strategizing to counterattack us. An adversarial search employs a strategy or policy instead of a sequence of activities. For instance, the agent does b if the opponent does a, the agent does d if the opponent does c, and so on. *Minimax Search* is the most popular term for adversarial search. This method is primarily employed to determine the optimum movements in games. This algorithm is currently utilized in two-player games such as *Tic-Tac-Toe* and chess as part of artificial intelligence. It makes use of the notion of a tree data structure. It goes through the tree and records every action that can be made in the game, where a player's gain or loss represents each move. The Minimax theorem by *Von Neumann* states that in these kinds of games, there is always a set of strategies that leads to both players gaining the same value and that one should employ this strategy set since this is the best possible value one can expect to gain, is the theoretical foundation upon which this search algorithm is founded [Nik+54]. This search's assumption that the opponent will behave in a way that effectively minimizes your profits and maximizes his own is one of its drawbacks. These, however, will only stand if your opponent is logical, experienced, and a fallible human. Sometimes, taking a chance and hoping your opponent doesn't see through a subtle countermove is better. Furthermore, representing every move in a primary game, such as tic-tac-toe, is relatively easy. Still, describing every move in a more complex game like *Chess* becomes computationally expensive. Because of this, programmers frequently use additional methods, like *Alpha-Beta Pruning*, to focus their search [KM75]. This entails halting the node's utility computation when it is ascertained that its value cannot possibly surpass that of a neighboring node. A different approach is known as the minimax approximation. Restricting the depth to a given point, treating the moves at that point as temporary terminal nodes, and calculating the values of those nodes using *Heuristics* are more methods of narrowing down the search space. Nevertheless, this presents a challenge when long-term planning is required [SB06]. However, this strategy can be strengthened by identifying stable game stages and utilizing them as intermediary terminal nodes [SK89]. Even with these methods, the effectiveness of using a minimax search in such complicated circumstances is debatable. The following section 3.3 covers multi-agent search to help you better grasp adversarial search.

3.3 Multi-Agent Search

Previous chapters have been devoted to single-agent search techniques. However, different contexts link several agents with the same issue, implying that multiple agents are interacting with one another. If agents are not functioning effectively, precise prediction activities might not occur. While some agents have goals and can benefit from other agents' actions, most multi-agent systems operate with incomplete knowledge. Because of this, surroundings of this kind are seen as unpredictable. *Multi-Agent Search* assigns a conflicting aim to multiple agents. These agents must contend with and strive to defeat one another to win the game. The adversarial search is given such an incompatible purpose.

When we talk about games, we usually mean ones that involve *Human Intelligence* and *Logic*, leaving out other factors like the link factor. The basis for these kinds of searches is the mathematical idea of game theory. *Game Theory* states that two players participate in a game. To compete, one must win the game; losses are inevitable for others [FT91]. Selecting the best method that yields the optimal result in the shortest time is always necessary. Multi-agent search issues require general techniques like *Pruning* and *Heuristic Functions* to satisfy their fundamental requirements. The key to pruning is a method that lets you ignore parts of a search tree that aren't needed for the desired outcome.

On the other hand, before reaching the destination node, the heuristic function permits approximating the cost value at each level of the search tree. A *Game Tree* is used during gameplay to help players identify all options and select the best one. The *Game Search* technique uses elements that include players, activities, outcomes, terminal tests, and utility during the searching process. The starting state of the game describes how it is configured at the outset. The player who has moved into the state space is then indicated. It returns the set of moves in state space that are allowed after specification. Then, it describes the outcome of moves made in the state space in the transition model. Define the move's outcomes in the search now. The game will continue as usual if it defines that it has ended and returns valid. Numerical values are what determine the outcome in the final component. For instance, it signifies -1 if the player loses, $+1$ if the player wins, and 0 if the game is tied. Another name for it is the *Payoff Function*. The game of chess would be an excellent illustration to clarify this definition. Chess falls within the category of competitive games. After this is understood, we can use chess as an example, explaining each phrase. In its initial configuration, the board, with every piece placed in its designated starting square, is known as the initial state. In this game, there will be two players. The collection of all conceivable moves each player can make with all their pieces is known as the actions. The results model determines the new state based on the action taken and the existing states. The apparent terminal test will determine whether a king is checkmated or not. Let's now attempt to comprehend the *Utility Function*. It takes more effort to understand this. We know the possible outcomes are win, lose, or draw, corresponding cost values of $+1$, -1, and 0. Given the player's present state, the utility function aims to play the game until the terminal state is reached to maximize its payoff and minimize the opponent's. We refer to this as the *Minimax Algorithm*. This is a fairly accurate illustration of the utility function's operation. It is observed that because there are millions of moves in a game of chess, the algorithm's depth is constrained; that is, the utility function stops working once the terminal state is reached. In an adversarial search, the players typically decide the outcome and how the game will play out. Thus, the following sections 3.3.1, 3.3.2, 3.3.3 cover some adversarial search algorithms.

3.3.1   MiniMax Game Tree Search

A decision-making method called the *Minimax* algorithm determines a player's best course of action in a *Two-Player Game*. The algorithm examines every move the player can make and every reaction the opponent can make to any given move. Then, presuming that both players are playing to their best abilities, it provides a score for each move based on how the game turns out.

The algorithm then selects the move with the player's highest score. The algorithm's two objectives—minimize the player's maximum potential loss and maximize the player's minimal possible gain—are the source of the name Minimax. Let's examine how the *Minimax Tree Search* method operates. The Minimax algorithm examines every action and response that can be made in the game tree. A tree structure depicting every game's move and response is called a game tree. Every node in the tree denotes a possible game state, and every edge denotes an action the player can take to get there. The Minimax method examines the tree recursively, beginning with the current game state. The program assesses every move the player can make at every given node and every conceivable reaction the opponent can make in response to each of those actions. Then, assuming that both players are playing to their best abilities, it rates every move that could be made about the game's result. The algorithm selects the move with the highest score if the present player is the one who is maximizing. The algorithm chooses the move with the lowest score if the present player is the one who is minimizing. The game's end is represented by a terminal node, which the algorithm reaches as it recursively explores the tree. The algorithm now returns the terminal node's score, which indicates the game's result. According to Figure 3.1, Assume we have the following move tree, where the values at the leaves indicate that the node is a square when it is the opponent's turn and a circle when the current player is moving. The values of the nodes one level above the leaves can now be filled in. At these nodes, the player in question moves. Since the player selects the best choice, the value will be the highest of its entire *Offspring*. Let's say, for instance, that we are at the level above the children and the far left node. The player can make one of two moves, resulting in a position with a value of -6 or a position with a value of 10. The player should choose the move that results in a position with a value of 10 because they wish to maximize their options. Because of this, the position's value is 10, indicating that the player made the best decision. It is the opponent's turn at these points, as indicated by the square nodes at the next level of the tree. Once more, the opposition has maneuver options. The child with the lowest value—the larger, the better for the player to move, and the smaller,

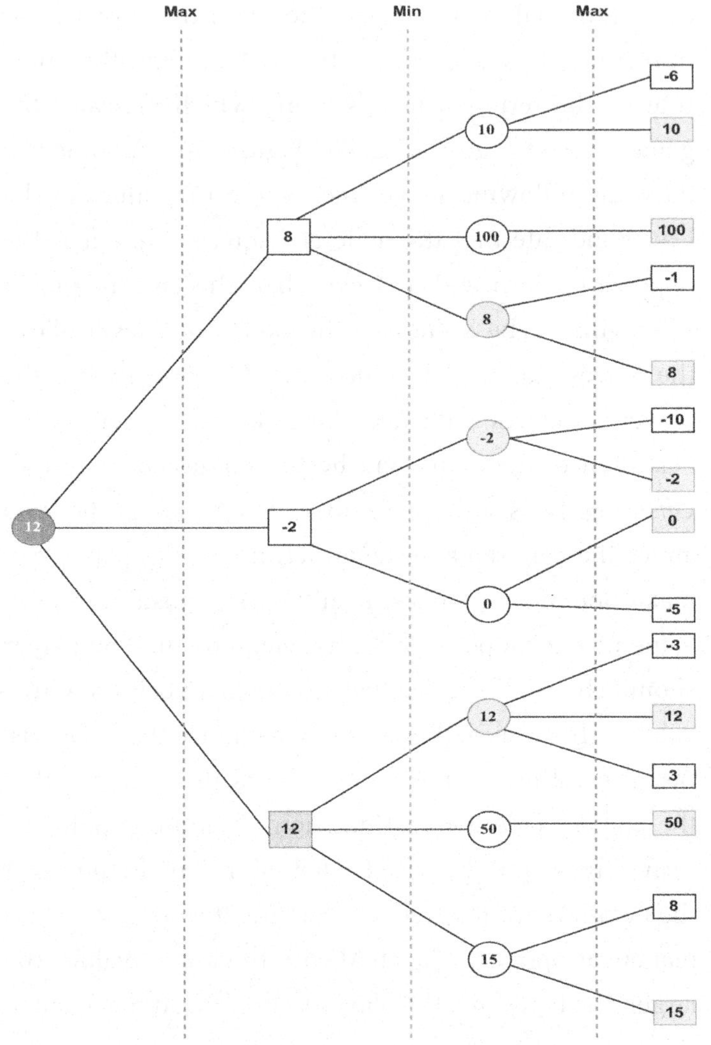

Figure 3.1: An Example of MiniMax Game Tree Search

the better for the opponent—should be chosen by the opponent since they want to use their best alternative. For instance, the opponent can move to spots valued at 10, 100, and 8 from the leftmost node at the current level. We presume they would do that since 8 is the minimum and the opponent's best option. As a result, the current node's value is 8. After finishing this level, the player advances to the next level, which is the root node. There are three possible moves: to places with values of 8, -2, and 12. Twelve is the value at the root since the player selects the best option. The player advances to the location corresponding to the maximum child, in this case, the rightmost child of the root. Next, it's the turn of the opposition. The technique is known as the *Minimax Algorithm* because it alternately maximizes and minimizes variables at different levels of the tree. The Minimax algorithm is an effective tool for determining decisions in two-player games. Assuming that both players are playing as ideally as possible, the algorithm can determine a player's optimal move by examining every move and answer and scoring each potential result. However, the approach may be computationally costly for big game trees with more nodes. The goals take a lot of work to accomplish. An alternative technique, such as the *Alpha-Beta Pruning Tree Search*, solves these issues.

3.3.2 Alpha-Beta Pruning Tree Search

In-game tree search algorithms, *Alpha-Beta Pruning* is mainly applied to minimax algorithms for making decisions in *Adversarial Games* like tic-tac-toe or chess. The goal of alpha-beta pruning is to increase the efficiency of the search by lowering the number of nodes in the tree structure that the minimax algorithm must assess. During the search process, the alpha-beta pruning algorithm monitors two parameters: α and β. The alpha value represents the best maximum score the maximizing player (e.g., $-\infty$) has found thus far. In contrast, the beta value represents the best minimum score the minimizing player (e.g., ∞) has seen thus far. The algorithm compares the alpha and beta values of the current node with the values derived from evaluating its child nodes as the search moves forward and evaluates an intermediate node in the game tree. The remaining sibling nodes can be eliminated if the alpha value is more than or equal to the beta value because they are unimportant to the outcome. This is because the player maximizing

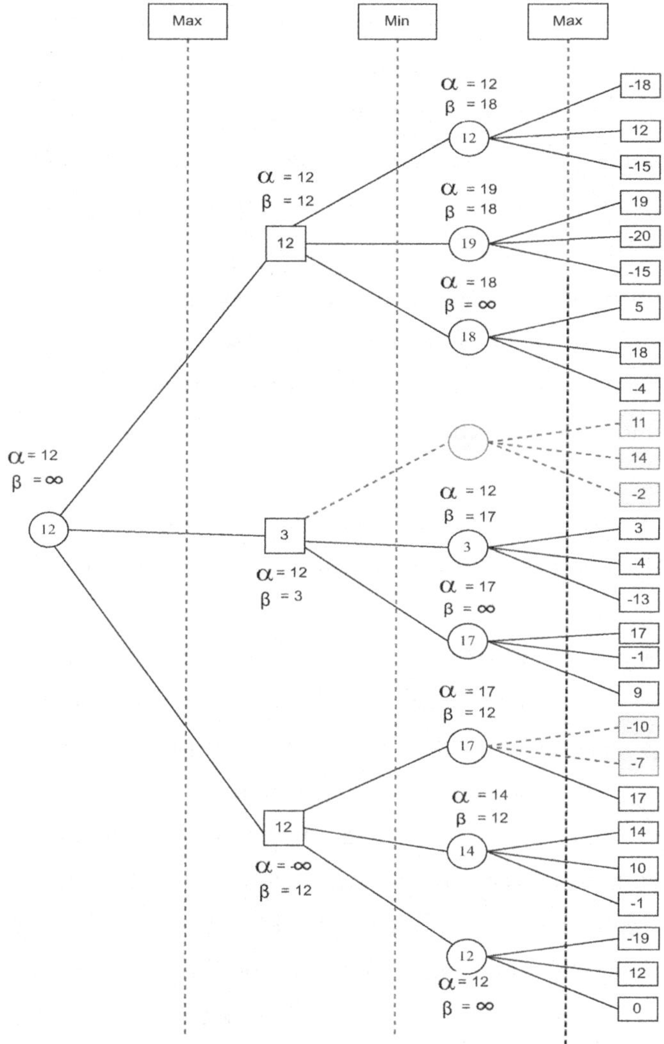

Figure 3.2: An Example of an Alpha-Beta Pruning Tree Search   125

or reducing has already discovered a better choice by taking a different route. Therefore, there's no need to waste computing power assessing those superfluous nodes. Alpha-beta pruning helps the search algorithm focus on the more promising branches of the game tree while ignoring larger areas of the tree. This reduces the search space and increases overall efficiency. It is an effective optimization method for sorting through the enormous array of movements and situations that can be made in competitive games. Here is a basic example from the Figure 3.2.

The minimax algorithm (Cf. Section 3.3.1) assessed the alpha-beta pruning search strategy. The maximum value was initially selected from the child nodes' bottom. A portion of the nodes' values are repeated during this process. Therefore, we eliminated these nodes until we found a quicker solution. For instance, node 17 repeated itself, removing parts of its child nodes. As such, the search process became more efficient whenever we eliminated redundant or undesired elements. The search tree's uniqueness is unaffected even if we eliminate parts that aren't needed. This method fits the majority of applications. Let's use chess as an example. Alpha-beta pruning is a method for making chess algorithms run more quickly. Chess programs work on the basic principle of creating a long list of all possible moves by you, followed by a long list of all possible moves by the other player for each item on the first list, and so on, for as long as you believe you have time. After evaluating each potential position, you work your way back to the beginning, presuming that each player chooses the option they believe to be best. When you occasionally get to the point where you can decide If the other guy is smart, he won't make that move, so I can skip checking what moves I could make after it, alpha-beta pruning comes into play. This is how the alpha-beta pruning facilitates process acceleration in chess-like games.

3.3.3   Monte Carlo Tree Search

The scientists who developed the *Monte Carlo* integration method used to visit a casino called Monte Carlo. In summary, the geometric area under the curves of the *Probability Distribution* statistics functions represents the concept of probability in statistics. Therefore, an analytical formula, or calculus, is used to find the area under the curve. However, if you don't have a formula, integrate the *Probability Distribution Function* or *PDF*. You can fit a PDF inside a bounding box that surrounds a specific area as long as you know the formula for the PDF. The optimal move in a game can be found using *Monte-Carlo Tree Search* or *MCTS*, developed using Monte Carlo methodologies. A search tree is utilized to arrange prospective moves, and numerous random simulations are employed to determine each move's long-term potential. It is a probabilistic and heuristic search algorithm that integrates machine learning principles of reinforcement learning with traditional tree search implementations.

Because MCTS is a method for making decisions in an environment where an agent interacts with it to maximize its rewards, it is regarded as a reinforcement learning component. A key component of *Reinforcement Learning*, in which agents learn to make successive decisions to maximize cumulative rewards, is using MCTS to search through potential actions and outcomes and identify the optimal path of action. Essentially, MCTS facilitates an agent's exploration and utilization of its surroundings to enhance decision-making abilities, a crucial aspect of reinforcement learning. It stimulates and assesses moves until they reach a terminal state, using a selection approach to identify the most intriguing moves to investigate further. The statistics acquired during the simulation phase determine the ultimate move. MCTS typically consists of four steps: *Selection, Expansion, Rollout* or simulation, and *Backpropagation.* Let's now examine the MCTS algorithm's operation. Determining the probability of the most likely winning

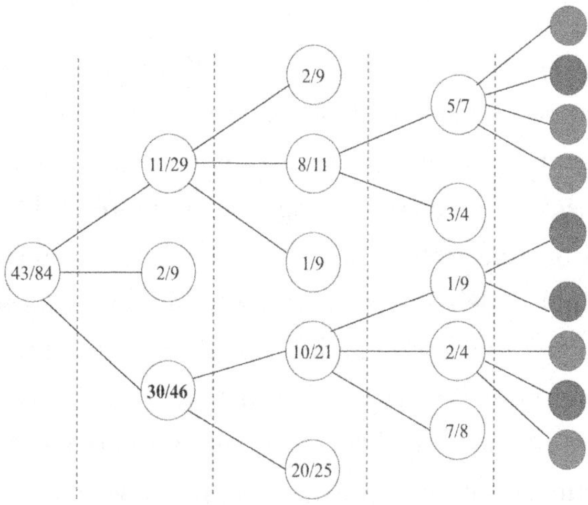

Figure 3.3: General Illustration of Monte Carlo Tree Search

node in each search tree branch is the primary goal of

this approach. According to Figure 3.3, blue signifies a lost game, and red indicates a win. Additionally, the probability of the heuristic values is shown for each node. For instance, 30/46 denotes that Red won 30 out of 46 games. Choose the best child node by applying the Equation 3.1, beginning at the root node.

$$\text{For all } i \max \left(V_i + \sqrt{\frac{C1 * \log(n)}{n_i}} + \ldots \right) \tag{3.1}$$

Where V_i represents the *Evaluation Function*, C1 indicates the current node, and $\log(n)$ represents the number of possibilities of the current node. The next step, expansion, involves creating one or more child nodes based on selection. In the third step of the simulation, the child node's insights can be found and used to win the game. Backpropagation can then be used up until the root node is reached. For instance, the values at the bottom of the blue child nodes are 3/4 and 5/7. Should we utilize backpropagation, parent node 8/11 will be obtained. Backpropagation was used in this manner up until the root node. Thus, this is how the MCTS methods function. In addition to being successful in numerous games, MCTS has also been used to solve other decision-making issues, including *Scheduling* and *Resource Allocation.*

3.3.4   AND-OR Search Tree

An *AND-OR Search Tree* is a pictorial representation of the reduction of objectives to unions and intersections of sub-objectives. AND-OR search trees often specify the space needed to solve a particular problem. There is a need for AND-OR search trees to implement common search strategies like *Breadth-First* (Cf. Section 2.3.1), *Depth-First* (Cf. Section 2.3.2), *Best-First* (Cf. Section 2.4.2), and others. This search approach can generate multiple nodes in parallel or sequentially, which produces one node at a time. A rooted, finite tree with AND and OR nodes is called an AND-OR tree. Meanwhile, the second player is to play in AND nodes, and OR nodes correspond to places with the first player. Except for the root node, every node has a parent. A directed edge is drawn between a parent and a child for every legal move. A description of the move, such as move coordinates, is labeled on each edge. Although it can also be an AND node in practice, the root is invariably an OR node. Every node in an AND-OR tree can have a value of win, loss, or unknown when viewed from the perspective of the first player. Nodes with uncertain values must be further investigated by expanding a subtree to ascertain whether the node is a win or loss with the best play. Node values such as win and loss show positions that are known wins and losses for the first player, respectively. An AND-OR tree is said to be solved when it has been established that the root node's value is either a win or a loss.

A leaf node at the terminal is childless. Depending on the game's regulations, it has a value of either a win or a loss. An internal node has at least one child. A node that is not terminal is referred to as a non-terminal leaf node. A leaf node's internal or terminal status is unclear. "K node has value x" can be shortened to "k node is x." The values of its children can be used to calculate the values of internal nodes. An internal OR node n is also a win if at least one of its children is a win because the first player can move to that child. If n has no children, then n is also a loss. Analogously, an internal AND node n is a win if all of its children are wins and a loss if at least one of its child nodes is a loss. A node shown to be successful is often referred to as a *Proven Node*, whereas a

node shown unsuccessful is known as a *Disproven Node.*
A calculated win is proof, whereas a computed loss is a
disproof. A *Proof Tree* is an AND-OR subtree that ensures
a node is proven by holding the winning strategy for
the first player. There are two definitions for a *Disproof
Tree,* which includes a winning strategy for the opposing
player. It has one child of an internal AND node, all
children of an internal OR node, and all terminal nodes
are losses. An example of an AND-OR tree is shown

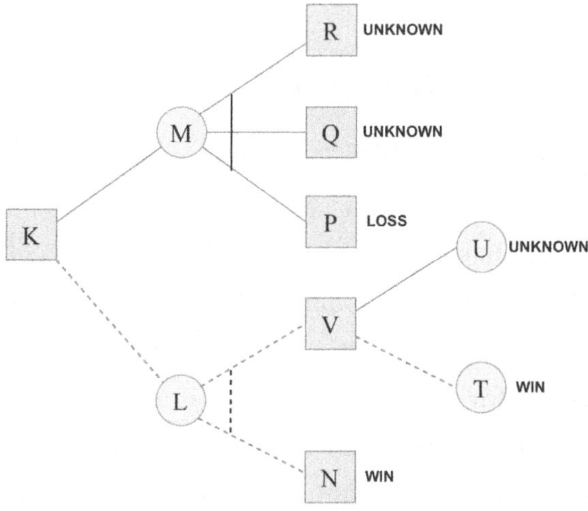

Figure 3.4: An Illustration of an AND-OR Search Tree

in Figure 3.4. AND nodes are shown as circles, and OR

nodes are shown as square boxes. The root node is node K. K, L, M, and V are internal nodes; N, P, and T are terminal nodes; Q, R, and U are leaf nodes with unknown values. By propagating backward the values of the leaf and terminal nodes, the values of the internal nodes are computed. T is a win, so V is also a win. P is a loss, so M is also a loss. L is a victory since N and V are wins, which makes K a win. There is a proof tree for K displayed with dashes. The AND-OR search tree space is valuable for many real-time applications, like *Video Games*.

3.3.5 SSS* Algorithm

We saw the *Alpha-Beta Pruning Tree Search* process in section 3.3.2, and in this section, we will talk about the tree that alpha-beta investigated. The *Binary Game Tree* is for deep play, and the dark nodes are the ones that the alpha-beta did not investigate. The alpha-beta algorithm now looks for an algorithm that is not ignorant, not blind in this sense, but has a sense of direction by searching from left to right. Consequently, we want to look at an algorithm that will essentially travel in the direction of what it believes to be a good solution, much as we went from *Depth-First Search* to *Best-First Search* by inserting *Heuristic Functions*. Stockman introduced this technique in 1979; it's known as *SSS**. To comprehend this algorithm, we must first identify the space in which the best first search will take place and examine the actions of max. Therefore, Max generally chooses one option out of several options in a game. Thus, while it appears to be making a decision, it is making a decision based on searching a key to a certain extent—let's use the example of a *n* play search—and Max has taken this action due to this look ahead. Additionally, it is based on using the evaluation function on the horizon. Thus, it can be said that Max has effectively anticipated or looked ahead at Min's reaction. Put another way, Max feels at ease with every response from Min, and for every one of those responses, Max has planned ahead, deciding to take a specific action before taking into account every response from Min.

Let's assume that a four-play search tree is given. Max has considered every option available to him and has essentially made the decision. You could, therefore, claim that the subtree we are currently viewing is what Max came to as a result of this search. If Max is going to make this move, then any move Min makes, Max has a response for that, and Max has taken that into account when assessing this. You will recall that this subtree type is a *Strategy*. Therefore, Max has selected a strategy. On the other hand, the alpha-beta method does not search in the space of strategies; in fact, it does not even consider strategies as such. However, the SSS* algorithm searches within the domain. Now, one question arises: what is the value of strategies? Usually, the value that Max has considered is in terms of the leaf nodes. Let us summarize this method: SSS* is a search method that performs a best-first state space search traversing a game tree, akin to the A* search algorithm (Cf. Section 2.4.3). The idea that solution trees are strategies is the foundation of SSS*. Any arbitrary game tree can be transformed into a solution tree by reducing the number of branches at each Max node to one. It identifies a maximum action for the opponent's potential combination of moves. Such a tree serves as a comprehensive Max strategy. SSS* analyzes larger and larger sub-trees as they progress through the space of partial solution trees, ultimately producing a single solution tree that shares the same root and Mini-Max value as the original game tree. SSS* may trim certain branches that alpha-beta pruning would not, but

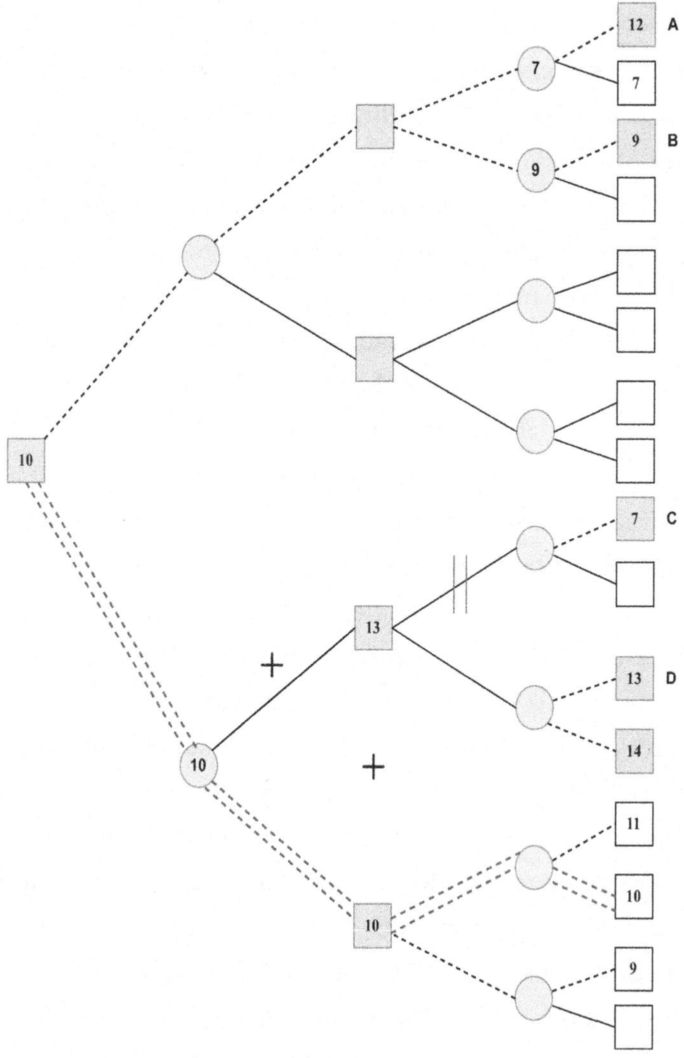

Figure 3.5: An Example of SSS* Search Tree
137

it never investigates a node it would prune. According to Stockman, alpha-beta may not be the best general algorithm, but SSS* might be. Let's now examine how the SSS* search algorithm operates. Every leaf node is a part of two strategies and operates according to a strategy(s). For instance, one strategy for Max could be that if Max moves, Min moves, and Max responds. As a result, Max looks ahead. Furthermore, the value of leaves needs to exceed the value of strategies(s). SSS* keeps track of the active nodes' descriptors in an OPEN list. As a priority queue, the descriptors are arranged in decreasing order of merit. As a result, it is an alpha-beta algorithm *Best First Variation*. Each leaf node is part of a group of strategies. As a result, the algorithm uses the alpha-beta approach to search through every strategy. To cover all strategies, first choose a set of leaves. This means it should take a subtree from the game tree, with the Max node selecting all branches and the Min node selecting only one. After that, maintain a priority queue of nodes representing *Clusters*. Next, until the ideal answer is identified, improve the partial solution method that seems the best. It should be emphasized that the issue is resolved when a root is tagged. Typically, SSS* goes through two search stages, such as the phase of node expansion and the phase of solution. While the solution phase focuses on the bottom-up search for the optimal Max strategy, the node expansion phase focuses on the top-down extension of a Min strategy. An illustration of the SSS* Search Tree method is shown in Figure 3.5. Four clusters of strategies—A, B, C, and D—are depicted in the figure of the sixteen available leaf nodes. Select the best cluster D after further refining the clusters. Following that, an algorithm uses a recursive call with an upper bound of 13 to improve cluster D. As a result, D is completely refined. The value 10 is the minimax at which SSS* ends. This algorithm has specific issues attached to it. Understanding the algorithm's operation and its relationship to alpha-beta requires significant work. SSS* also keeps an OPEN list data structure comparable to those in single-agent search algorithms like A*. The list's size increases exponentially as the search tree gets deeper. Numerous scientists have come to the conclusion that SSS* can never be truly useful for real-world applications, such as game-playing software. Furthermore, the OPEN list needs to be maintained in a sorted fashion. Inserting and deleting operations on the OPEN list will take up most of any application that uses SSS∗ execution time. Even though SSS* promises to expand fewer nodes, its drawbacks discourage the practical application of the technology.

3.4 Applications

3.4.1 Chess Game

The world's most brilliant brains have been playing *Chess* for decades, and it's a cognitively demanding game. Thus, how can a computer be trained to play a cerebral game like chess? Let's now examine how an AI chess game operates. Typically, the procedure consists of five steps. The procedure starts with move generation and board visualization. It essentially puts all of the chess rules into practice. Determine all permitted movements for a specific board condition based on these guidelines. The board state primarily utilizes common mathematical functions to determine the optimal movements. In some AI environments, the board condition can determine the outcome of a solid game. The evaluation of one's position is the second step in this process. Generally, an algorithm determines the stronger side in a given situation. This can be done to determine each piece on the board's relative strength. The *Evaluation Function* provides the greatest evaluation values, which aids in determining the relative strengths of the pieces on the board. The third phase of the procedure uses Minimax (Cf. Section 3.3.1) to generate a search tree when the position evaluation is finished. The *Minimax Algorithm* explores the recursive tree of all potential moves to a predetermined depth and evaluates the location of the tree's ending leaves. Next, depending on whether the child is a white or black node to move, it returns either the greatest or the smallest value to the parent node, attempting to maximize or reduce the result at each level. The primary limitation of the minimax algorithm is its significant dependence on the tree's search depth, which determines the algorithm's efficiency. The fourth phase of solving the issue is *Alpha-Beta Pruning* (Cf. Section 3.3.2). We can ignore some search tree branches with this algorithm optimization technique. This aids in thoroughly evaluating the minimax search tree with the same resources. If a move we uncover results in a worse scenario than one we have already found, we will cease examining that portion of the search tree. Furthermore, it just speeds

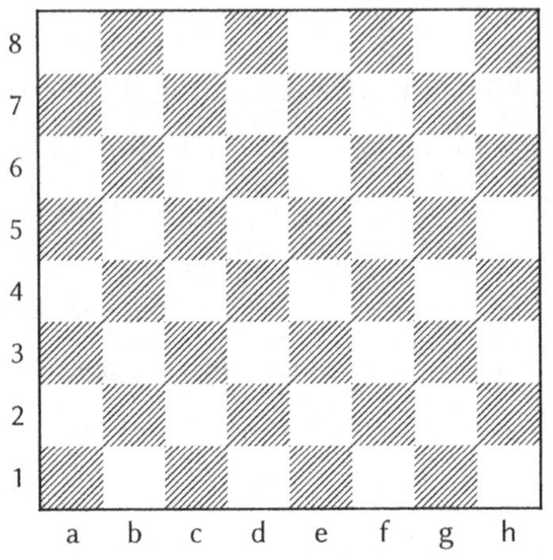

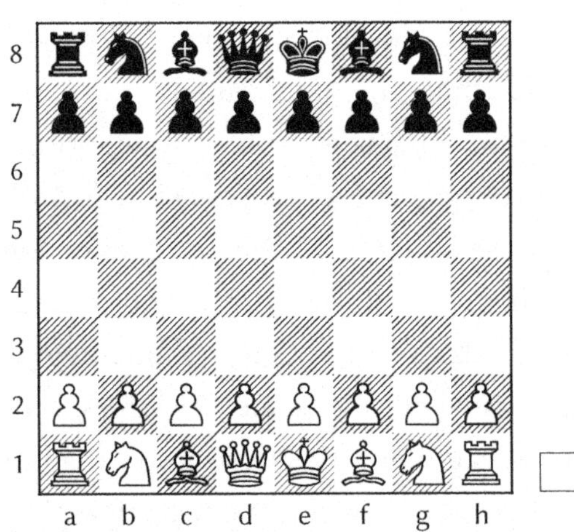

Figure 3.6: General Representation on Chess Board

up the minimax algorithm without changing its result. The fifth phase of the process, the *Evaluation Function*, may need to be improved in particular circumstances. Because it just counts the information on the board, the first evaluation function is rather basic. To improve this, include a factor in the evaluation considering the pieces' positions. For instance, a knight in the middle of the board is superior to one on the edge since it has more possibilities and is more active. The general layout of chess boards is shown in Figure 3.6. Playing a decent game of chess requires a little improvement. However, difficult problems in *AI-Chess* applications include move ordering, faster generation, and end-game-specific evaluation.

3.4.2 Checkers Game

AI is used in games to enhance search, knowledge, and heuristics. Comprehending AI and games is critical since they offer a sandbox to evaluate search engines' effectiveness. It is also a way to comprehend how complicated games are. Arthur Samuel, an early pioneer in AI and machine learning, did some of the earliest work enabling computers to learn from experience. Apart from training the *IBM-701* computer to play *Checkers*, he also invented the concept of allowing the software to learn by competing with itself [Sam59]. The next Checkers program participated and triumphed over the country's fourth-ranked player. Because of the significance of Arthur Samuel's checker's program for non-numerical computing, additional logical instructions were incorporated into the early IBM computers by design. The first program to triumph against a human in the machine world championship competition is the Checkers program, developed at the University of Alberta in Canada.

A computer software called *Chinook* plays checkers. In the field of Checkers AI, Samuel's work is still relevant, but *Neural Networks* has been used more recently. The *Anaconda Checkers* player was designed with an evolutionary strategy, which means genetic algorithms evolve the neural network's weights when sufficient information is provided to comprehend the game's permissible plays. The outcome was a Checkers player defeating a commercial Checkers program 6 to 0. Regarding the pieces required to play and the rules that apply, checkers are far simpler than chess because checkers have two types of pieces, whereas chess has six pieces. In addition, each player in Checkers only has

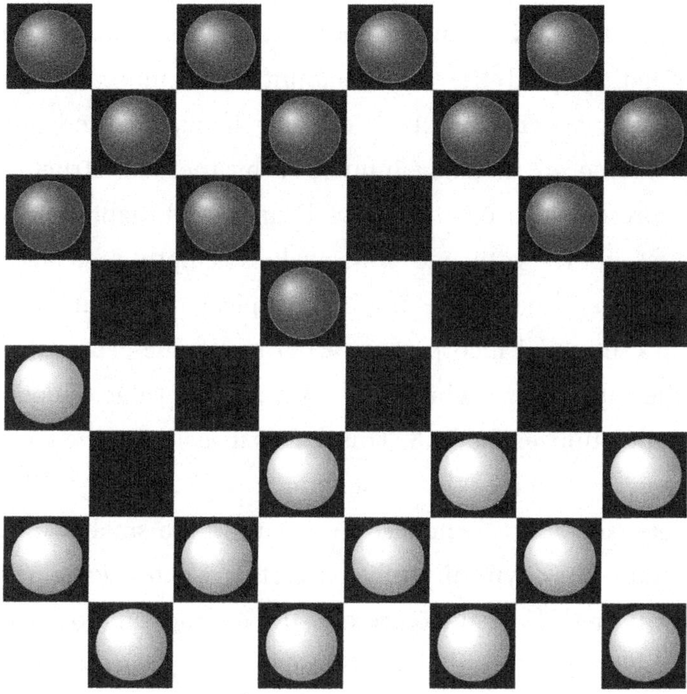

Figure 3.7: Basic Illustration on the Checker Board with Checkers

access to half of the board—that is, 32 square rather than 64, illustrated in Figure 3.7. Checkers is more complicated than Chess (Cf. Section 3.4.1) despite being simpler overall. Let us see how the AI in Checker portrays the board and engages in sophisticated gameplay. The efficiency of the program's search and evaluation functions and the total amount of memory utilized by the search game tree, opening book, and endgame database are strongly influenced by the data structure representation of a checkers board. A straightforward 8×8 matrix with one of six values—empty, red, black, red-king, and black-king—is a typical depiction. The 10×10 model incorporates a border of one cell around the entire board, which contains the static value offboard and optimizes the 8×8. This makes it easier for the move generator to recognize unlawful moves. Although other representations condense the board into a smaller form factor, they typically rely on certain *Central Processing Unit* or *CPU* architecture and the instructions to query and control the individual bits. Checkers programs share several characteristics with other AI players, like chess programs, such as having distinct game phases at the beginning and conclusion. We'll see parallels between Checkers and Chess software because of this. Many studies have examined opening plays that can result in advantageous board configurations because Checkers has been extensively explored theoretically. Typically, searching through a database of opening moves yields the first set of moves for a given strategy, after which search and evaluation procedures control piece movement. A weighted numeric feature vector is typically used as the board evaluator. The number of red pieces, number of black pieces, and the disparity of pieces, which means the number of red pieces minus the number of black pieces, the number of red kings, and so on, are examples of specific properties.

Although it is possible to modify the weights automatically (i.e., the evaluation function is no longer static), a human expert often adjusts the weights. Chinook's evaluation function is defined by 22 weighted characteristics. Usually, the feature weights are adjusted by hand. The game tree is searched using minimax with alpha-beta pruning (Cf. Section 3.3.2), just like in most classical games. Compared to Chess, Checkers has a lower average branching factor of 10, but it is still high enough to make it impossible to search the entire tree. Although alpha-beta pruning effectively minimizes the search tree, heuristically applying additional strategies might further reduce the search space of the game tree. Several search upgrades, such as windowing, can speed up game tree searching by using the alpha and beta bounds as a window of the already computed values. *Principal Variation Search* or *PVS* is another enhancement that adds windowing to every node in the game tree. A hash table that preserves board configurations and their properties is built throughout gameplay to expedite the search. Since specific boards may appear repeatedly throughout a game, scanning the specific subtree can be minimized by storing them along with the alpha and beta parameters corresponding to them from the minimax tree. The board configuration can be quickly looked up using the hash table to determine if it has been seen before. If so, the alpha-beta search uses the returned alpha and beta parameters. *Zobrist Hashing* is a popular hash function in Checkers hash tables [Zob90]. The *Checkerboard* is XORed by this *Hash Function*, producing distinctively different hash values for various board configurations. This is required for quick hash storage and lookup to guarantee a hit. A relationship between board configurations with a few pieces left, and the winning strategy can be found in an end-game database. These databases, which are usually compressed, encapsulate the board compactly and then employ an index function to determine the appropriate strategy swiftly. All eight-piece board variations, or about 444 billion configurations, are included in the Chinook end-game database. The run-length encoding of the end-game representation is used to compress the database.

3.4.3   Go Game

Generalized Opponent Artificial Intelligence or *Go-AI* is a sophisticated and advanced idea that centers on developing clever computers to win challenging games, especially the age-old board game Go. Beyond conventional AI techniques, Go-AI aims to develop agents that compete with human players and outperform them in the game. It is important to comprehend the significance of Go as a game before diving into Go-AI. Go is an abstract strategy board game that is thought to have originated in China more than 2500 years ago. It is also known as Baduk in Korea and Weigi in China. It first became quite popular in Asia and then expanded to other parts of the world. Go's basic principles, arranging black and white stones on the grid to encircle opponents' territory and capture their stones, give rise to the game's complexity (see Figure 3.8). It's an incredible challenge for AI since there are an infinite number of conceivable combinations on the board—more positions than atoms in the universe. Games have always fascinated AI, even in its early development stages. One of the first games that AI could win was chess, where major achievements were made when IBM's *Deep Blue* beat World Chess Champion *Garry Kasparov* in 1997. But because Go has such a large search area, it turned out to be a far more difficult problem for AI, which helped to advance deep learning and neural networks. In recent years, deep learning and *Neural Networks* have changed the capabilities of AI. *Deep Learning* uses neural networks to automatically learn hierarchical representations from raw data, like photographs or board positions in the game of Go, instead of depending on human-generated characteristics. This methodology has demonstrated remarkable efficacy across multiple domains, including natural language processing and computer vision [Sil+16]. The introduction of *AlphaGo* by DeepMind, an AI research facility under *Alphabet*

Inc., Google's parent company, in 2016 marked a turning point for Go-AI [Cha+16]. With the victory over professional human go player Lee Sedol—a well-known South Korean player with many world titles—AlphaGo became the first AI computer to achieve this feat. This triumph demonstrated the ability of deep learning to master challenging games and signaled a significant advancement in AI capabilities. AlphaGo's advanced

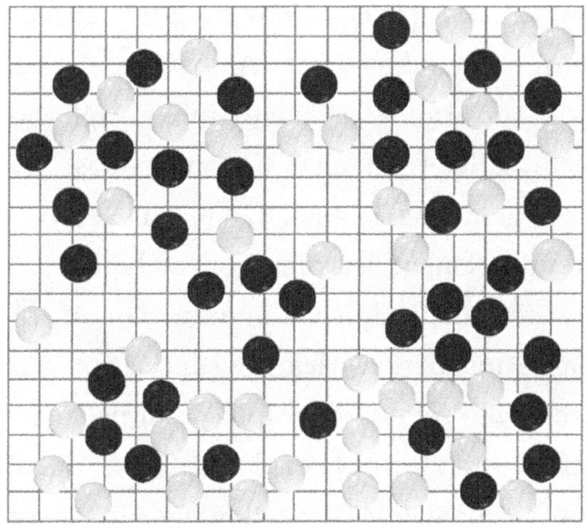

Figure 3.8: General Illustration of the Go-AI game

architecture is responsible for its success. It brought

together several neural network models, such as a value network, a policy network, and an algorithm called *Monte Carlo Tree Search* (Cf. Section 3.3.3) or MCTS. To make strategic decisions, MCTS effectively explored the game tree. The policy network projected the optimum movements in a given position, and the value network estimated the possibility of winning from a particular position, and so on. Although AlphaGo was revolutionary, DeepMind didn't stop there. They unveiled AlphaGo Zero in 2017, exhibiting an even more astounding feat. AlphaGo Zero began the game without prior knowledge, unlike AlphaGo, which picked up skills from elite human games. It played millions of games against itself to teach itself completely, using reinforcement learning to get better. AlphaGo Zero outperformed AlphaGo in days, demonstrating the potential of unsupervised learning and self-play in Go-AI. The success of DeepMind's AlphaGo project encouraged other AI research teams to explore GO-AI. AlphaGo Zero (100-0) and AlphaGo Master following AlphaGo's victory over Lee Sedol, DeepMind kept pushing the envelope. In 2017, they unveiled AlphaGo Master, which pulled off an incredible win over the top-ranked Go player in the world, *Ke Jie*, in a three-game battle. This demonstrated that AlphaGo had truly attained superhuman abilities and that its success wasn't a fluke. DeepMind also disclosed that an improved *AlphaGo Zero* had defeated the previous iteration of AlphaGo with an astounding 100-0 record that same year. This performance cemented GO-AI's reputation as one of the most important advances in AI research by demonstrating the enormous progress gained quickly. Even while GO-AI's main goal has been to win the game of Go, its achievements have far-reaching effects off the board. The methods and strategies created for GO-AI have been used in various fields, such as robotics, finance, healthcare, and more. The noteworthy accomplishments in GO-AI have also spurred conversations regarding the moral implications of AI research. Concerns over AI systems' possible effects on society, the labor market, and human-AI relationships grow as they gain strength. For AI to be developed and used responsibly and ethically, it must be ensured to maximize advantages and minimize problems.

3.4.4   Poker Game

AI has long been a part of two-player zero-sum games like Chess, Checkers, and Go, as covered in the previous sections 3.4.1, 3.4.2 and 3.4.3. *Game Theory* was the foundation for each AI software created for these games, which all sought to approximate the *Nash Equilibrium* somehow [Van91]. AI programs are capable of beating even the best poker players. For better understanding, the various forms of Poker cards are illustrated in Figure 3.9. Because some of the cards being played are hidden, making it more difficult for anyone to predict how the hand will turn out, it is a game of imperfect information. Computer programmers used to have to implement systems based on flawed methods like the *Monte Carlo Simulation*, Nash equilibrium, and *Bayes Theorem* because of this lack of information. Instead of trying to assess every play until the end of the game, *Pluribus*, the master of poker, needed to see a few steps ahead to decide what to do. For instance, both players can see the pieces on a board and determine the next move that they or their opponent can make. AI has taken advantage of the fact that an opponent may make a surprise move, but it must be lawful to reduce the

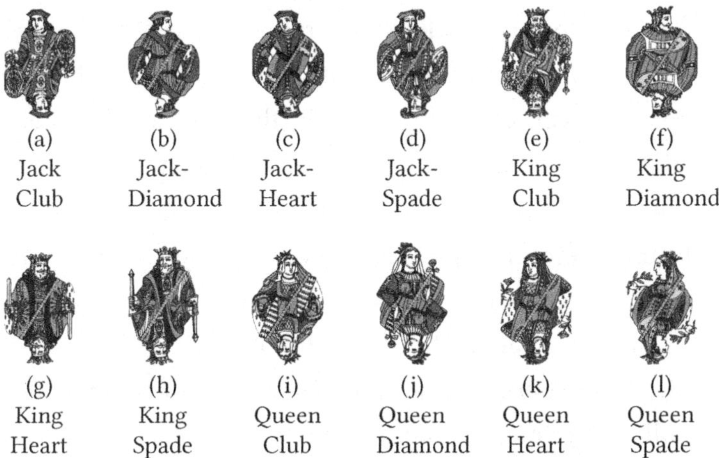

Figure 3.9: Various Forms of Poker Cards

element of uncertainty. To put it more clearly, in poker, players must use intuition to determine which cards their opponent is holding in their hand because neither of the other players knows what the other player is playing with. AI frequently uses algorithms to determine every outcome that could occur in a game, which can result in the emergence of ineffective strategies. *DeepStack* is one of the two systems that have ultimately defeated a human poker player. A major factor in their success has been allowing the AI to only calculate a few steps ahead of time and to recalculate data as new information is added to the game. The program has been able to reduce the number of possible scenarios by learning and adapting to the behavior in the game, thanks to the creation of *Neural Networks* via machine learning. An estimated 10 million randomly generated poker game scenarios had to be solved before DeepStack's neural network could be trained. The bots had to learn the poker rules to compete against real players, who typically play in groups of more than two. To the best of our knowledge, there are three different kinds of AI systems for poker: Pluribus, DeepStack, and *Libratus*. Let's start with Pluribus; this game was created to be played against copies of itself without any data or human input beforehand. It began to play from the beginning, minimizing counterfactual regret. This became an iterative process whereby the game learned and stored knowledge about many possible strategies. The longer it played, the better the results because it could determine which techniques worked and which didn't. When playing against actual poker players, Pluribus employed built-in learning software to learn from its opponents and adjust its approach after using its stored data as a guide to begin the game. Part of what allowed Pluribus to defeat players—poker champions, no less—in a six-player match was its capacity to adapt, learn, and employ various tactics as the game progressed. The second kind of poker software is called DeepStack. It was recently tested over four weeks against 33 professional poker players, playing nearly 40,000 no-limit, two-player Texas Hold'em games. Researchers calculated that the AI had a final win rate of 486 million big blinds per game after eliminating cases of winning by sheer luck. This is almost ten times more than a skilled professional poker player would consider a good rate. It was able to accomplish this, in part, because of technology that was integrated into the game. It allowed the strategies and probabilities to be updated anytime new information was introduced, such as a new card or wager. To aid in its learning while it plays, DeepStack also includes deep learning software. The third kind of Poker program is called Libratus. Libratus, created by Carnegie Mellon academics, participated in a 20-day poker tournament and won after 120,000 hands, defeating four of the best human poker players. Because Libratus lacks learning software, unlike DeepStack, it needs a lot more processing power to run its algorithms and does not improve over time. Even though AI has advanced significantly as technology has progressed, it will take some time before these bots completely dominate poker games or even significantly impact the game itself [BS19]. Only recently have algorithms been created to outperform humans at chess, a game where artificial intelligence has been developed for years. Even in this case, competitors still greatly value human interaction in the game. Poker is a game where telling and bluffing are still essential. A strong player is not only determined by their hand strength but also by their style of play, when they fold, the size of their bets, and their ability to display emotion. The *Psychology* and socialization at the base of poker are two components of the game that the algorithms are still learning. Without having to risk real money, AI can assist players in learning new tactics and enhancing their poker skills.

3.5 Summary

In AI, adversarial search is a crucial method for decision-making in a competitive scenario where competing agents have divergent objectives. It uses game trees as a standard representation to assess and decide on the optimal move while considering opponents' actions and countermoves. The multiple-agent search environment presents in-game applications like poker, go, checkers, and chess. The game-playing environment's result is determined using the minimax technique. It does not support large branching factor trees. Hence, Monte Carlo tree search is utilized to get around the issue. In addition, the alpha-beta pruning tree approach removes unnecessary portions of branching trees. This fundamental idea of adversarial search helps decision-making, strategic planning, and gaming in various contexts.

3.5.1 Multiple Choice Questions

Exercise 1: Which search matches the MiniMax search while removing the branches that do not affect the outcome?

a) Monte carlo tree search

b) Alpha-beta pruning

c) Hill-climbing search

d) Simulated annealing

Exercise 2: Which algorithm decides whether to win or lose a game tree?

a) Breadth First Search

b) Heuristic Search

c) MiniMax Search

d) Greedy Search

Exercise 3: Which of the searches is closest to MiniMax?

a) Greedy Search

b) Depth First Search

c) Breadth First Search

d) Hill-Climbing search

Exercise 4: Which environments use adversarial search problems?

a) Cooperative Environment

b) Competitive Environment

c) Neither Competitive nor Cooperative Environment

d) Competitive and Cooperative Environment

Exercise 5: Which of the following is not part of the Monte Carlo tree search process?

a) Collection   b) Expansion   c) Vision   d) Scope

Exercise 6: Which of the following AI-game applications is too complicated to beat?

a) Chess   b) Checkers   c) Go   d) Pokers

Exercise 7: Poker is a single-agent game. State whether it is true or false

a) True   b) False

3.5.2 Short Answer Type Questions

1. Identify the elements of the game-playing approach in adversarial search.

2. How does exploration differ from exploitation?

3. State the purpose of utility function.

4. Express how alpha-beta pruning tree search is utilized in large search trees and give a suitable example.

5. Define AND-OR search tree and where it can be deployed.

6. Why are probability distributions given more priority in the game of checkers?

7. Analyze the purpose of Go game.

8. Summarize the characteristics of the SSS* algorithm.

3.5.3 Long Answer Type Questions

1. Explain the AND-OR search tree algorithm with a suitable example. State the limitations of the algorithm.

2. Discuss the role of MiniMax algorithm in game tree search.

3. What are the search-related similarities between Go game and Chess? Provide a suitable strategy for playing these games based on those differences.

4. Briefly illustrate the fundamental working procedures of Alpha-Beta pruning tree search with a suitable example.

5. Give a brief example demonstrating the steps involved in Monte Carlo tree search procedures.

Chapter 4

Propositional Logic

4.1 Goal of the Chapter

The preceding chapter 3 covered adversarial search in relation to various game-playing applications, including checkers and chess. Because the issue domains of these applications are stated as a simple graph, they are not the best fit for vast, uncertain AI environments. Knowledge-based strategies like propositional logic are applied to solve this issue. In an uncertain AI world, it concludes the information and acts rationally. Thus, propositional logic's basic mathematical ideas and related methods will be covered in this chapter.

4.2   Introduction

Propositional logic is a branch of mathematical logic that looks at how statements are related logically. It gives the tools to create and study computer systems and programs. *Propositions*, either true or false statements, are the building blocks of *Propositional Logic*. Logic operators like negation, conjunction, disjunction, conditional, and bi-conditional can join propositions to make them more complicated[End01]. You use your username and password to log in to a website. The computer first turns the password that was entered into a hash value. It then searches the database for a username. If the username is not in the database, it shows "false." If it is, it shows "true." The hash result is True if they match and False otherwise. Propositional logic can also be used to check if an argument is deductively valid instead of inductively valid, which is how most people think in real life. Propositional logic doesn't tell us if the propositions are true or false. Instead, it tells us if the conclusion comes from the *Premises* (if the premises are true). In this case, it's still essential to have the subject knowledge to figure out whether a politician's claim is true or false.

If the politician makes a leap in logic from the evidence not supported by the truth conditions of propositional logic, you can use propositional logic to show that their case is wrong. Studying and using logic helps you make intelligent decisions, think clearly, and draw consistent conclusions. One question comes up: what does logic have to do with AI? It's the same as how *Reasoning* and *Natural Intelligence* work together. Any mind needs to be able to use logic. The amount of analysis determines whether it is enough. Our knowledge often doesn't make sense, but that's because we only know how our brains work. Many people think our brains are like *Artificial Computers* made by natural selection. But we need to find out how they work. Thus far, it has yet to be shown that they can do anything our future artificial computers cannot do. There is no way to make our artificial computers do anything but be rational. There are times when mathematicians must think about *Propositional Reasoning*. Once they've learned them well enough, they follow *Logical Rules* without thinking about it. But we need to write down the rules to make the proof of the theorem automatic. After that, *Propositional Calculus* is a vital part of the scheme. Logic is sometimes thought of as getting the correct new sentence when given other lines. Propositional logic, which doesn't look inside a simple sentence, does this. Instead, it provides symbols for the most straightforward sentences from natural languages that are true and other symbols for adverbs and conjunctions that combine these sentences logically in natural language. These are all important reasons why propositional logic is so important in artificial intelligence when concluding an environment that isn't stable.

4.3   Fundamentals

In AI, an intelligent agent must know about the natural world to make good decisions and act quickly. It usually has two main parts: the *Knowledge Base* and the *Inference Rules.* There are a lot of sentences that make up knowledge, but inference rules are used to get new rules from old ones. Now, there's a question. What are sentences, and how do they help an AI agent make decisions? The answer is *Propositional Logic* or PL. It is a logical language that uses logic to connect statements and symbols to stand for *Propositions.* Some letters, like *P, Q,* and *R,* are used in propositional logic. These letters are called propositions, and logical connectives like *Conjunction*($\wedge$), *Disjunction*($\vee$), and *Negation*($\neg$) join them. A disjunction joins two propositions by the link *OR*, while a conjunction comprises two propositions by the link *AND*. Negation is all about reversing the statements shown as *NOT*. This organized representation is beneficial because it lets AI systems use the information to think, conclude, and make intelligent choices. Each proposition in propositional logic is a fact or a claim about the world. For example, the sentence "Earth is an oblate spheroid" is a true proposition. On the other hand, "8 + 3 = 14" is a proposition that stands for a false statement. These claims can be written in many ways, such as English sentences, math equations, or computer statements. Eight plus three equals fourteen, and "Earth is an oblate spheroid." Which of these statements should you consider as a whole to decide if it's true or false? In this way, the propositions determine what to do. *Logical Connectives* are used to join propositions together so that more complicated statements can be made, which is very helpful in unstable decision-making environments. *Truth Tables*, on the other hand, show the truth values of statements and the logical connectives that link them. The logic that only deals with true or false statements is called propositional logic. *Syntax* and *Semantics* are the two main components of propositional logic, which are covered in the following sections 4.3.1 and 4.3.2.

4.3.1   Propositional Logic Syntax

The formal rules for making *Well-Formed Formulas* or WFFs in *Propositional Logic* are laid out in the syntax of propositional logic. Propositional logic is a branch of logic that looks at claims that can be true or false. A *WFF* is a statement that can have a truth value put on it. For

Table 4.1: Propositional Logic Formulas

1	The words *true* and *false* are formulas.
2	All propositional variables that say something are formulas
3	$\neg P$ is a formula for every formula P.
4	$(P \wedge Q)$ and $(P \vee Q)$ are formulas for all formulas P and Q.

example, the letters P, Q, and R represent propositional variables, the basic building blocks of propositional logic. To make a WFF, combine propositional variables with logical connectives (Cf. Section 4.3.3). This is how the set of formulas in propositional logic is defined inductively, as illustrated in Table 4.1. The phrase $(P \wedge Q)$ means that

Table 4.2: Examples of Well-Formed and Not Well-Formed Formulas

Well-Formed	Not Well-Formed
R	PQR
$\neg\neg R$	$(R$
$(\neg(P \vee Q))$	$\vee Q$
$((\neg P \vee Q) \wedge R)$	$\neg\vee\wedge$
$\neg((\neg P \vee Q) \wedge R)$	$P \wedge P$

the conjunction of P and Q, $(P \vee Q)$ means the disjunction of P and Q, and $\neg P$ means the negation of P. When we read $\neg P$, we mean "Not P." When we read $P \wedge Q$, we mean "P and Q." and also we read $P \vee Q$, we mean "P or Q." Because of the braces around conjunction and disjunction, each string of symbols made by the above definition can only be read as a formula in a single way. We usually leave out the last set of brackets when we write formulas. For example, we write $P \wedge (Q \vee R)$ instead of $(P \wedge (Q \vee R))$. A syntax tree can show formula P, Q, and R. The nodes inside the tree are named after connectives, and the leaves are named after propositional variables. The size of P equals the number of nodes in its parent tree. Each node in the syntax tree determines a

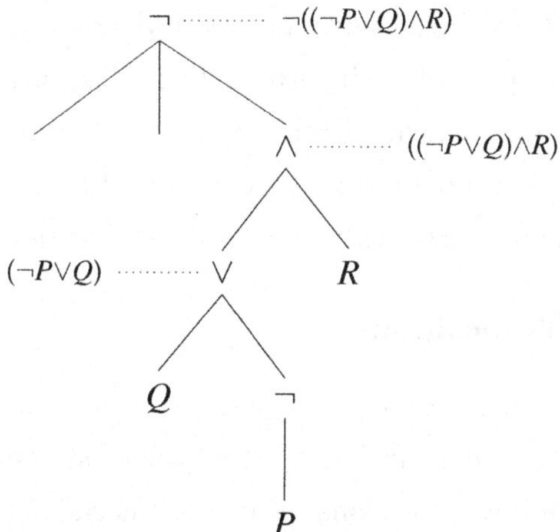

Figure 4.1: ¬((¬P∨Q)∧R) Syntax Tree

part of *P*, whose *Syntax Tree* is the part of the tree that starts at that node. Let's say that $\neg((\neg P \lor Q) \land R)$ is a statement. It has sub-formulas called *Q*, *R*, *P*, $\neg P$, $(\neg(P \lor Q))$, $((\neg P \lor Q) \land R)$, and $\neg((\neg P \lor Q) \land R)$. Figure 4.1 shows $\neg((\neg P \lor Q) \land R)$ syntax tree. This is possible because the set of propositional formulas is structured to let us define functions on those formulas by induction. Here are some examples of well-formed formulas and formulas that aren't well-formed that are illustrated in Table 4.2. An atomic proposition and a compound proposition are the two main parts of the syntax of propositional logic.

Atomic Propositions

The idea of an atomic proposition is one of the most fundamental ideas in logic. One type of statement can't be broken down into smaller ones. It is called an *Atomic Proposition*. A letter or a number, like *P*, *Q*, *R*, or *S*, can represent an atomic statement. For example, "the sun is hot" is an atomic proposition, while "the sun is cool" is not. The statement can also be reckoned to be either true or false. In some cases, the statements itself can tell you the facts. Say something like, "The cat is on the mat." This statement may be true or false based on

Table 4.3: Atomic Propositions with Fact

Atomic Proposition	Fact
P: Thiruvarur is in Tamilnadu	TRUE
Q: The grass is green	TRUE
R: Sun rises in the east	TRUE
S: Apples are oranges	FALSE
T: The sky is blue	TRUE
U: 2+5=7	TRUE
V: The sun is hot	TRUE
A: Grapes are brown	FALSE
Y: Sun sets in the west	TRUE
M: Tamilnadu is in India	TRUE

where the cat is. In the same way, "The car is red." This is indeed true if the car is red. Statements that are atomic propositions and not atomic propositions are shown in Tables 4.3 and 4.4. Even though atomic propositions

Table 4.4: Not Atomic Propositions with Fact

Not Atomic Proposition	Fact
P: Do you speak Tamil?	Question
Q: Close the window	Command
R: You were amazing!	Exclamation
S: This sentence is false	Inconsistent
T: $x > 10$	Predicate

are more straightforward, they can be helpful in some of the more complicated cases of artificial intelligence for representing information and *Automating Reasoning*. Sometimes, it is beneficial to determine whether the software is correct. Because of these things, atomic statements are critical in propositional logic.

Compound Propositions

Compound propositions combine one or more atomic propositions using logical connectives and parentheses. That is, propositions with some connectives are called *Compound Propositions*. Use capital symbols like P, Q, R, S, and more to show a compound proposition. One example of a compound statement is "sun rises in the east and sunsets in the west." whereas "sun rises in the east, sunsets in the west" is not a compound proposition. In the same way, "Thiruvarur is in Tamilnadu and Tamilnadu is in India" is a compound statement, but "Thiruvarur is in Tamilnadu, Tamilnadu is in India" is not. Table 4.5 shows statements that are compound propositions and their propositional logic translations. The following Section 4.3.2 addresses the *Semantics* of propositional logic, which describes how to assign well-

Table 4.5: Compound Propositions with Propositional Logic Translation

Atomic Proposition	Compound Proposition	Translation
P: It is raining today	It is raining today and street is wet	$P \land Q$
Q: Street is wet	It is raining today or street is wet	$P \lor Q$
	It isn't raining today and street is wet	$\neg P \land Q$
	If it is raining today then street is wet	$P \to Q$
	It is raining today if and only if street is wet	$P \leftrightarrow Q$

formed formulas truth values.

4.3.2   Propositional Logic Semantics

The semantics of propositional logic tell us how to assign well-formed formulas or *WFF* truth values. Truth statement functions map to each propositional variable, either true or false. Then, the truth value of a WFF is found by evaluating the truth values of its logical connectives to those of its variables. So, the WFF $P \land Q$ has a truth value if and only if both P and Q are true. Truth tables (Cf. Section 4.3.4) show the truth value of a WFF by listing all the possible truth assignments and the truth value that comes from them. Usually, when we think of propositional variables, we think of sentences that can be true or false. What does a proof system do?

Regardless of the factors, it tells us what propositional formulas must be true. Truth is a semantic idea that gives meaning to specific terms. Use the letters P, Q, and R to separate propositional variables from arbitrary formulas and X, Y, and Z to separate arbitrary formulas from propositional variables. One example is the function f that has $f(P) = \text{T}$, $f(Q) = \text{F}$, $f(R) = \text{F}$, and $f(S) = \text{T}$. This function is a truth assignment for the set of variables P, Q, R, S. A truth assignment describes a possible state of the world. First, the letters are shorthand for the sentences in Table 4.6. The first and third claims

Table 4.6: A Typical Example of Truth Assignment

Statement No.	Variables	Truth Assignments
1	P:	Rohit brother was the victim
2	Q:	Rohit was the killer
3	R:	Rohit was in the bar

are usually true, while the second is false, as indicated by the answer to the simple *Puzzle*. Truth assignment gives P and R the value T and Q the value F. We can turn a truth assignment function f into a valuation function $\bar{f}$ by adding a set of *Propositional Variables*. This function then gives every propositional formula that depends only on these variables a true or false value.

The function $\bar{f}$ is defined recursively, meaning formulas are evaluated from the bottom up. This means that the value given to a compound formula is based on the values given to its parts. These are the most critical parts of propositional logic. These types of *Semantic Notion* logic help AI find malicious actors in environments that aren't stable. More complex logic, like predicate and model logic, is built on top of propositional logic. These logics let you consider objects, their properties, necessity, and possibility. Besides this, the next Section 4.3.3 talks about logical connectives.

4.3.3   Logical Connectives

AI uses logical connectives to combine one or more simple atomic propositions so that it can think about the world in a more complicated way. Using connectives, we can also make compound statements. Connectives like negation, conjunction, disjunction, implication, and biconditional are often used. The logical connectives are briefly discussed in the following subsections.

Negation

One way to change the truth value of a statement is to use the *Logical Connective Negation*. The symbol ¬ indicates the NOT operator or negation. For example, an atomic statement is "P: The sun is hot," and the negation is "¬P: The sun is not hot." Truth tables (Cf. Section 4.3.4) are used to see which of the various truth assignments to propositions is the best. Besides this, a truth table is a tool that helps us understand how the truth values of different statements change when different logical connectives link them. The table 4.7 shows the truth values of statements when they are negated.

Table 4.7: Negation Truth Table

P	¬P
TRUE	FALSE
FALSE	TRUE

Conjunction

The AND operator connects two or more propositions, as the symbol shows ($\wedge$). If P and Q are two prepositions, then the conjunction $P \wedge Q$ is only true if both P and Q are true. For example, if P stands for "Thiruvarur is in Tamilnadu," Q for "Tamilnadu is in India." $P \wedge Q$ is only true if both "Thiruvarur is in Tamilnadu" AND "Tamilnadu is in India" are true. Table 4.8 shows the truth values of two proposition variables in *Conjunction*.

Table 4.8: Conjunction Truth Table

P	Q	P∧Q
TRUE	TRUE	TRUE
TRUE	FALSE	FALSE
FALSE	TRUE	FALSE
FALSE	FALSE	FALSE

Disjunction

The OR operator connects two or more propositions, as denoted by the symbol $\vee$. Let's say that P and Q are two propositions. The *Disjunction $P \vee Q$* is true if at least one of the statements it connects is true. If P stands for "Thiruvarur is in tamilnadu," and Q for "Tamilnadu is in india," then $P \vee Q$ is only true if either "Thiruvarur is in tamilnadu" OR "Tamilnadu is in india" OR both are true. Table 4.9 shows the truth values of two proposition variables in disjunction. There are two kinds of OR: inclusive($\subseteq$) and exclusive($\oplus$). In an exclusive OR, if $P \wedge Q$

Table 4.9: Disjunction Truth Table

P	Q	P∨Q
TRUE	TRUE	TRUE
TRUE	FALSE	TRUE
FALSE	TRUE	TRUE
FALSE	FALSE	FALSE

is true, then $P \vee Q$ is false. For example, every natural number is either even or odd, but never both. In other words, every natural number is either even or odd. For an exclusive OR to work, only one of its reasons must be true, not both. An inclusive OR is true if any of P, Q, or $P \wedge Q$ is true. Indian citizens are usually vegetarian or non-vegetarian. However, many of them are vegetarian and non-vegetarian, which is called inclusive OR.

Implication

The implication logically depends on the first proposition; the second proposition is linked to the first by an assumption. A connection between two statements, P and Q, is shown by $P \rightarrow Q$. This can also be written as "if P then Q" or "P implies Q." P is what came before Q, and Q is what happens after P. The implication is false only if P is true. That's the best meaning of the word "implies." It is pointed out that *P* and *Q* may be separate and unrelated propositions. In Table 4.10,

Table 4.10: Implication Truth Table

P	**Q**	**P→Q**
TRUE	TRUE	TRUE
TRUE	FALSE	FALSE
FALSE	TRUE	TRUE
FALSE	FALSE	TRUE

see the truth values of two statement variables that are *Implications*. For example, look at the sentence, "It's raining, so it must be cloudy." In the traditional way of reasoning, this only means that it is not true right now that it is raining and not cloudy. The sentence talks about the weather at the moment. It doesn't mean that rain makes it cloudy. Even though cloudiness has generally been linked to rain, it's common to think of these as the meaning of casual discussion.

Biconditional

The symbol ↔ represents a *Biconditional* implication, meaning it can go either way. It can also be written as "if and only if." Also, both $P{\rightarrow}Q$ and $Q{\rightarrow}P$ put together.

For example, "the Scotland will play in the cricket world cup if and only if they win the world cricket league." Let *P* mean "the Scotland will play in the cricket world cup," and *Q* means "They (the Scotland team) win the World Cricket League." Then, we can write $P{\leftrightarrow}Q$. We can be sure that Scotland will play in the Cricket World Cup if we believe this statement is true and they win the World Cricket League. But it also says that Scotland must have won the World Cricket League if they will play in the World Cup. It works both ways. The biconditional implication is the name for this. Table 4.11 shows the truth values of two proposition variables that depend on each other. Regarding AI, the *Propositional Model*

Table 4.11: Biconditional Truth Table

P	**Q**	**P$\leftrightarrow$Q**
TRUE	TRUE	TRUE
TRUE	FALSE	FALSE
FALSE	TRUE	FALSE
FALSE	FALSE	TRUE

assigns each proposition a truth value. In case you forgot, propositions are statements about the world that can be true or false. On the other hand, the truth values of these statements show what we know about the world. The model is the assignment of truth value that tells us about the world. Let's say *P* is "Thiruvarur is in Tamilnadu," and *Q* is "Tamilnadu is in India." Then, the following truth-value assignment could be a model: P=True, Q=False. Based on this model, Thiruvarur is in Tamilnadu, but Tamilnadu is not in India. In this case, though, more theories could work. In the case of P=True, Q=True, both Thiruvarur and Tamilnadu are in India. There are twice as many models as proposals. We had two propositions, which means there were two times four different models. It is a list of sentences that a knowledge-based agent knows. The AI is given information about the world through propositional logic statements that it can use to draw more conclusions about the world.

4.3.4   Truth Table for Compound Propositions

Truth tables list all the possible combinations of inputs and outputs based on a condition, such as if outputs are fed to an AND, OR, NOT, or other function. This logical math process is helpful in many areas; T and F can be written as 1s and 0s, and the correct answer can be reached by changing the inputs to the outputs. Let's look at a truth table with three statements in Table 4.12 as *P*,

Q, and *R*. This *Truth Table* shows three statements called

Table 4.12: Truth Table With Three Propositions

P	Q	R	P∧Q	P∨R	(P∧Q)↔(P∨R)
T	T	T	T	T	T
T	T	F	T	T	T
T	F	T	F	T	F
T	F	F	F	T	F
F	T	T	F	T	F
F	T	F	F	F	T
F	F	T	F	T	F
F	F	F	F	F	T

propositions, whose letters are *P*, *Q*, and *R*. There are three columns, each listing all the possible truth values for propositions *P*, *Q*, and *R*. The truth values for the statement "P∧Q" are shown in the fourth column. This statement is only true when both *P* and *Q* are true (Cf. Table 4.8). There are truth values for the statement "P∨Q" in the fifth column. This statement is only false when *P* and *Q* are false (Cf. Table 4.9). The truth values for the statement "(P∧Q)↔(P∨R)" are shown in the sixth column. This statement is only true when both (P∧Q) and (P∨R) are true. In addition, this is only false if both (P∧Q) and (P∨R) are true (Cf. Table 4.11). We can quickly find out the truth value of a compound statement by looking at the truth values of its statements.

4.3.5   Tautology

In propositional logic, a tautology is not an atomic proposition; it can only be combined. It's said that a compound statement is always true if it always comes out true, no matter how the truth values of its parts are set. Let's look at the same example in Table 4.12 and how the logical connective changes from biconditional to an implication. From Table 4.13, in the sixth column, the

Table 4.13: A Typical Example of Tautology

P	Q	R	P∧Q	P∨R	(P∧Q)→(P∨R)
T	T	T	T	T	T
T	T	F	T	T	T
T	F	T	F	T	T
T	F	F	F	T	T
F	T	T	F	T	T
F	T	F	F	F	T
F	F	T	F	T	T
F	F	F	F	F	T

statement "(P∧Q)→(P∨R)" is only false when "(P∧Q) is true and "(P∨R)" is false. This is why we have tautologies.

The word *Tautology* comes from logic, about how ideas are put together, not what they say. This means that if you said, "I am young and confident," it would follow the same logic: "P∧Q" For the first case, *P* meant "I am young," and for the second, *Q* meant "I am confident." Since both claims are logically true, they are tautologies. A tautology is a form of logic that can never be false. Look at this sentence again: "I am confident and not confident." This is shown as P∨¬P in formal logic. In fact, this is true for all statements that end in "*P*" or "¬P." There is still a truth in P∨¬P, even if *P* is false. This is because "¬P" is true if *P* is false. This is how the knowledge-based agent learned and concluded that the claims were true.

4.3.6   Contradiction

There is a contradiction when there is a false statement, no matter what its variables are set to. There are an unlimited number of contradictions that can be found. This is shown in *Formal Logic* as P∧¬P. In reality, this is false for all statements that start with P∧¬P. When *P* is false, ¬P is true, so P∧¬P is still false. But when *P* is true, ¬P is false. This is known as a *Contradiction*. Let's look at the same example in Table 4.13 to see how the logical connectives change from $\rightarrow$ to $\wedge$ and $\neg$. The sixth column shows in Table 4.14 that the truth values for "$\neg(P\vee R)$" are reversed. They are shown in the seventh column. The statement "$(P\wedge Q)\wedge\neg(P\vee R)$" is only true when both $(P\wedge Q)$ and $\neg(P\vee R)$ are true. If not, it's false. That's why we have a contradiction. We use contradiction to find the truth

Table 4.14: An Example of Contradiction

P	Q	R	P∧Q	(P∨R)	¬(P∨R)	(P∧Q)∧¬(P∨R)
T	T	T	T	T	F	F
T	T	F	T	T	F	F
T	F	T	F	T	F	F
T	F	F	F	T	F	F
F	T	T	F	T	F	F
F	T	F	F	F	T	F
F	F	T	F	T	F	F
F	F	F	F	F	T	F

in the real world. In court, a guy says, "I don't drink whiskey, so I never buy it." The lawyer then shows the court a picture of the man leaving a store with the exact whiskey bottle that he used to hit his mistress. The man then says, "Myra died while I was driving with my cousin that day." Then, the lawyer shows a camera video from a neighbor that shows the man's car outside her house the day she was killed. He says, "My cousin was growing bananas, and he dropped the pot." The lawyer then shows a family ancestry that shows all of the man's cousins have died. Hence, this is a contradiction. So that we can better understand, let's say you did the crime while you were also with your friends out of town. In this way, you were in two places at the same time. This makes no sense. That means our first assumption was false. In real life, this is also known as a contradiction.

4.3.7   Logical Equivalence

Logical Equivalence is a connection between two compound propositions in propositional logic. This means that both statements have the same truth value in all situations. The ":$\Leftrightarrow$" symbol or "if and only if" shows this connection. In other words, two compound propositional expressions are logically equivalent if they are always true or always false with each other. If two or more statements are neither a tautology (Cf. Table 4.13) nor a contradiction (Cf. Table 4.14), this is called a *Contingency*. A tautology and a contradiction are parts of every sentence in classical reasoning. There are no logical differences between tautologies or contradictions.

In this case, *P* would be "Rajendra Prasad was the first Indian President," and *Q* would be "Abdul Kalam was the 11th Indian President." This phrase is turned into a propositional formula, written as P∧Q. "Abdul Kalam was the 11th Indian President," and "Rajendra Prasad was the first Indian President." It turns this statement into a propositional formula, Q∧P. In propositional logic, there are different ways to say the same thing. For any propositions *P* and *Q*, we had to write that P∧Q :⇔ Q∧P. For example, "P∧Q is logically equivalent to Q∧P." "¬(P∨Q)" and "(¬P)∧(¬Q)" are also logically the same.

Table 4.15: General Example of Logical Equivalence

P	Q	R	P∧Q	(P∨R)	¬(P∨R)	(P∧Q)∧¬(P∨R)	¬(P∨R)∧(P∧Q)
T	T	T	T	T	F	F	F
T	T	F	T	T	F	F	F
T	F	T	F	T	F	F	F
T	F	F	F	T	F	F	F
F	T	T	F	T	F	F	F
F	T	F	F	F	T	F	F
F	F	T	F	T	F	F	F
F	F	F	F	F	T	F	F

Table 4.15 also shows that (P∧Q)∧¬(P∨R) is logically the same as ¬(P∨R)∧(P∧Q), which means

that $(P \wedge Q) \wedge \neg (P \vee R) :\Leftrightarrow \neg (P \vee R) \wedge (P \wedge Q)$. Also, some mathematical expressions are considered equal because $x + y$ always equals $y + x$. Logical equivalence is essential in artificial intelligence because it makes complicated notions easier to understand and helps an AI agent think more clearly about the world.

4.3.8 Operators Property

Operators are used in propositional logic to combine propositions to make more complex propositions. In propositional logic, these are some of the things that operators usually do. To better understand operators' properties, let's use the universal set U={2, 4, 6, 8, 10, 12, 14, 16, 18, 20, 22, 24, 26, 28, 30, 32} and its three sets, P={4, 8, 12, 16}, Q={6, 12, 18, 24}, and R={8, 12, 24, 32}, to show and apply all of their logical properties.

Commutativity

According to the *Commutative* property, the result is the same no matter what order the operators are used in. Here's an example: P∨Q={4, 6, 8, 12, 16, 18, 24} is the disjunction of *P* and *Q*. It's the same as Q∨P={4, 6, 8, 12, 16, 18, 24}. The property also holds for P∧Q= Q∧P.

After this, the disjunction and conjunction operations are commutative.

Associativity

The associative property says that the result is not affected by how the operators are grouped. *P*, *Q*, and *R* are all joined together when (P∧Q)∧R={12}∧{8, 12, 24, 32}={12} and P∧(Q∧R)={4, 8, 12, 16}∧{12, 24}={12}. This means that the conjunction operation is *Associative*. The property also holds for (P∨Q)∨R=P∨(Q∨R).

Identity Element

It says that there is an element that can be put together with any other element using the function, and the result will not change. For example, P={4, 8, 12, 16}∧{2, 4, 6, 8, 10, 12, 14, 16, 18, 20, 22, 24, 26, 28, 30, 32}={4, 8, 12, 16} is the disjunction of *P* and the universal set {2, 4, 6, 8, 10, 12, 14, 16, 18, 20, 22, 24, 26, 28, 30, 32}. P={4, 8, 12, 16}∨{2, 4, 6, 8, 10, 12, 14, 16, 18, 20, 22, 24, 26, 28, 30, 32}={2, 4, 6, 8, 10, 12, 14, 16, 18, 20, 22, 24, 26, 28, 30, 32} works the same way. As a result, the *Identity Element* of the conjunction and disjunction operators is the universal set.

Distributive

One operator can be spread out over the other by the *Distributive* property. As an example, the conjunction operator gives more than the disjunction operator. In other words, $P \wedge (Q \vee R) = (P \wedge Q) \vee (P \wedge R)$. $P \wedge (Q \vee R) = \{4, 8, 12, 16\} \wedge \{6, 8, 12, 18, 24, 32\} = \{8, 12\}$, and $(P \wedge Q) \vee (P \wedge R) = \{4, 8, 12, 16\} \wedge \{6, 12, 18, 24\} \vee \{4, 8, 12, 16\} \wedge \{8, 12, 24, 32\} = \{8, 12\}$. The property also holds for $P \vee (Q \wedge R) = (P \vee Q) \wedge (P \vee R)$.

Demorgan's Law

DeMorgan's Law says that the negation of the disjunction between two sets P and Q is the same as the conjunction of the negations of P and Q. In other words, $\neg(P \vee Q) = (\neg P) \wedge (\neg Q)$. $\neg(P \vee Q) = \neg\{4, 6, 8, 12, 16, 18, 24\} = \{2, 10, 14, 20, 22, 26, 28, 30, 32\}$, and $\neg P \wedge \neg Q = \{2, 6, 10, 14, 18, 20, 22, 24, 26, 28, 30, 32\} \wedge \{2, 4, 8, 10, 14, 16, 20, 22, 26, 28, 30, 32\} = \{2, 10, 14, 20, 22, 26, 28, 30, 32\}$. In the same way, $\neg(P \wedge Q) = (\neg P) \vee (\neg Q)$ also meets the rule. That's why DeMorgan's Law is true.

Double Negation Elimination

An acceptable rule of replacement is double negation elimination, which says that if $\neg\neg P$ is TRUE, then P is

TRUE. If P={4, 8, 12, 16}, for instance, then $\neg\neg P$={4, 8, 12, 16}, which is the same as *P*. So, *Double Negation* elimination is still TRUE.

4.3.9 Canonical Forms

As a mathematical expression, canonical form is a common way to show that a mathematical object exists. It usually gives an expression's most unique representation and recognizes it specially. This term makes sense when there is more than one acceptable way to describe expressions. Any unique representation can be a *Canonical Form* [Min12]. Use the strings 04339 248363, +91-04339-248363, and +91.04339.248363 as examples. Our real-life experience tells us they belong to the same phone number in different formats. It's clear from the context that the first one is from India, even though it doesn't have the country code. But they are highly different for a computer program (Assume an AI Agent). Selecting a format might not matter if we only store it in a database to show it to others. Sticking to a unique representation is helpful if we want to look for them, call them, or do any automated task (Assume an AI Agent). Your method for the data will determine which format you choose and which the standard becomes. In some cases, it may only be considered an official one. To begin with, the file should have all the necessary data, including the country code. However, it's possible that storing the country code would be too much for your program; later, the format should adapt to growing needs and changing scope. Changing an existing database will be difficult if you have a list of phone numbers that only work in India and want to call other countries. The style should be simple to understand. For some reason, you may store numbers in a list that looks like [363, 248, 43, 39], but a new employee will need help understanding it, and your brain will have to make the changes from the forms it's used to. When we used letters instead of numbers, we lost the beginning zero. The format needs to work for a specific purpose. For sorting and searching, you might want one that uses strings with a fixed length, like "04339248363." Remember that the country code shouldn't have any zeros, but it can be written in a standard way. For example, the format should be able to be changed to binary for storage or text for human viewing. Everything has a unique standard form, which is what matters. You can also easily understand a boolean function's standard form. No matter how complicated a *Boolean Function* is, the canonical form of uniqueness can describe it. With the unique canonical form, an AI agent can quickly find unique content in an extensive database, which means that the level of complexity is significantly reduced. However, complexity is the major disadvantage of the canonical form boolean function.

4.3.10 Propositional Logic Limitations

Modern *Propositional Logic*, or PL, is part of a long history that goes back to *Aristotle* and back and forth. His syllogisms were great for making arguments that fit in first-order or *Predicate Logic*. As Aristotle himself said, "Socrates is a man, and all men are mortal. Therefore, Socrates is mortal." Then, syllogistic logic became the basis for *Euclidean* mathematics and some of the best logic in the middle period [Pat13]. Modern propositional logic doesn't easily accept these cases that use quantifiers like "all," "some," and "none." *George Boole*'s "Laws of Thought" was another development in the middle period. They were based more on math and polynomials than on Aristotle. Today, computer science and logic circuit design can only be done with Boole's work [Boo21]. It's an essential part of modern logic and is the same as propositional logic. With the idea of *Relational Predicates*, there is a real rule between propositional logic and the real quantifier logic of Frege and Russell [Hoc87; Mac05]. In elementary school, we learned about relations like "greater than," "less than," and "equal to." However, it took a lot of work for syntactical and semantical theory to figure out how to make sense of relational expressions. This is similar to plain logic, which is different from vector logic. Aristotle only used one quantifier in his logic based on a single predicate. In modern predicate logic, you can use as many *Quantifiers* as possible. The way you arrange quantifiers with logic operators changes what the statement means. Logic only works with statements that are either True or False, but there are limits to what can be put into simply propositional logic. Some good arguments can't be put into pure propositional logic. The premises are "All cats like running" and "Manas is a cat." The conclusion is "Manas likes running." This is a proper argument, but it would take a more complex logical system to make it work in another language.

Predicate logic, with the universal and existential

quantifiers, would be the framework needed. The argument would be given its sentence letters in propositional logic. Still, it would be False by truth table (Cf. Section 4.3.4) or derivation because P, Q does not always mean R. Also, PL needs to handle necessity and possibility. Seven plus seven must equal fourteen, so if it has to be done, it can be done. PL by itself does not allow this kind of logic. Neither do many other types of logic. The main idea is that logic, especially PL shows a formal reason, but there are other ways to reason. In logic, meaning is different from syntax, so a logical system needs to have suitable operators to handle different meaning problems and data. PL doesn't have much going on and can't explain some of its issues well. In PL, for example, a conditional statement with a false antecedent is always true, even if the antecedent is true. This is because of how the rules are written in the system. Also, *Contradictions* (Cf. Section 4.3.6) can mean anything in PL, so logic with more than one value could explain or allow that. It might seem like a T and F statement to say someone is bald after cutting their hair. This means that statements could be T and F, neither T nor F, or one or the other. So, it's clear that PL has some limits when using logical operators and symbols (Cf. Section 4.3.3) in the real world. Propositional logic also needs help with showing complicated connections between items or notions. It can only make straightforward propositional claims that have truth values of either true or false. It is hard to show ideas like vagueness, uncertainty, and ambiguity because of this. In addition, it doesn't make it easy to show negation. This can make it hard to show negative comments and give good reasons for them. It's hard to show recursive logic in forms like trees and lists, often used in AI applications. It has trouble with temporal aspects and changes over time, which is essential for many AI uses. In general, propositional logic helps you think about the calculations you can only do with AND($\wedge$), OR($\vee$), and NOT($\neg$). You need quantifiers or predicate logic instead of propositional logic if you need a loop or repetition, like FOR ALL($\forall$), THERE EXISTS($\exists$), While, Do-While, and more. Besides, these challenges are dealt with by AI using the advanced methods described in the following sections 4.3.11 to 4.3.16.

4.3.11 Handling Complex Knowledge: Probabilistic Logic

Some of the most advanced AI methods, like probabilistic logic, are used to solve uncertainty problems in the real world without enough information. According to this way of representing knowledge, the level of uncertainty in knowledge is shown by *Probability*. *Probabilistic Logic*, like *Bayesian* [Ber19] and *Markov Logic Networks* [RD06], takes the descriptive power of *Predicate Logic* and adds it to *Probabilistic Logic*. It can be used to show uncertain information, which makes it worthwhile in real life, where understanding is often based on probabilities. In uncertain logic, the statements are usually precise. There is no doubt about what the statement means. We are still determining the exact truth value of that statement; all we have is an idea of how likely it is to be true or its chance. Remember that every claim is true or false, never something else. An example of a real-life situation is "A match played between two teams." Another is "It will rain today." And a third is "It is likely that Dube is hungry." We can guess these statements will happen, but we're still determining, so we use probabilistic logic.

4.3.12   Handling Complex Knowledge: Fuzzy Logic

Fuzzy Logic builds on propositional logic to handle knowledge that isn't always precise. There are only two truth values in logic: false and true. Fuzzy logic is just those two truth values mixed together. Its degree of truth goes from false (0) to true (1) and stays that way. Like, 0.9 is kind of like "90% true." It needs to make rules about what "AND($\wedge$)" and "NOT($\neg$)" mean, and there are a few transparent ways to do this. Dr. Lotfi Zadeh of the University of California at Berkeley first developed the idea of fuzzy logic in the 1960s. Dr. Zadeh was working on the problem of how to make computers understand natural words [Zad96]. Usually, it takes work to translate everyday words into absolute numbers like 0 and 1. It's interesting to think about everything that can be summed up in two words, but a lot of the information given to computers is somewhere in the middle, and so are the effects of computing a lot of the time. It is helpful to think of fuzzy logic, as usually we think of binary or *Boolean Logic* as just one example. Complex information that needs clarification is directly incorporated into logic, which is how people think. *Cognitive Science* also uses it to determine if people think that way and what that means for how we work. In fuzzy logic, the propositions themselves are only sometimes clearly stated. One typical example is the sentence "To be tall." There's a chance that this condition has some truth values. Someone 3.60 meters tall needs to be qualified, and someone 0.56 meters tall needs to be qualified, too. But what about someone 1.84 meters tall? The domains of the predicates are no longer precise, exact, or fuzzy. This lack of precision runs through the whole reasoning. The main idea behind fuzzy logic is that it allows for some inconsistency when the third is unclear and some "open universe" when the third is not excluded. This can make the reasoning appear very subtle in what it means. Fuzzy logic is a key part of giving AI human-like abilities, also known as *Artificial General Intelligence*, which represents generalized human thinking abilities in application so that the AI system can figure out how to do something it hasn't done before. Overall, fuzzy logic is integral to artificial intelligence because it helps us deal with imprecise data and make decisions in complicated and uncertain environments.

4.3.13 Handling Complex Knowledge: Predicate Logic

Predicate logic, also known as *First-Order Logic,* adds quantifiers, predicates, and variables to propositional logic to make it more helpful in representing knowledge in complex environments. In propositional logic, the truths of the natural world can be easily shown as well-formed formulas for local statements (Cf. Section 4.3.1). It is also used a lot in AI systems that use symbols. More information about the predicate logic will be discussed in the following Chapter 5.

4.3.14 Handling Complex Knowledge: Description Logic

Description Logic or DL is a group of structured languages and reasoning systems that describe and alter complicated notions, and it defines how they formally relate to each other. To make it work, it represents a set of concepts, relationships, and axioms that govern how these concepts and relationships work with each other [Baa+17]. Then, it uses *Automated Reasoning* algorithms to conclude this knowledge base. DL is linked to first-order logic (Cf. Chapter 5), but its syntax is more limited, which makes it better for automated reasoning. DL makes it easy for computers to understand, represent, reason, and change structured, complex knowledge. It can be used in areas like knowledge representation, natural language processing, ontology engineering, knowledge management, the semantic web, and machine learning. In *Knowledge Representation*, for instance, DL can be used to put an expert's environment knowledge into a form that computers can understand. AI programs can also use this information to decide what to do or answer questions. When knowledge representation is used in DL, the frame problem and the computational complexity are issues. This area of AI study has an optimistic future, and DL looks incredibly interesting.

4.3.15   Handling Complex Knowledge: Ontologies

Ontology is a group of rules describing knowledge in large and complicated domains. *Web Ontology Language* or *OWL* is often used to show it. It uses classes, individuals, and properties to organize information beyond propositional logic. For instance, the approach shouldn't describe the cat and its specific traits. Instead,

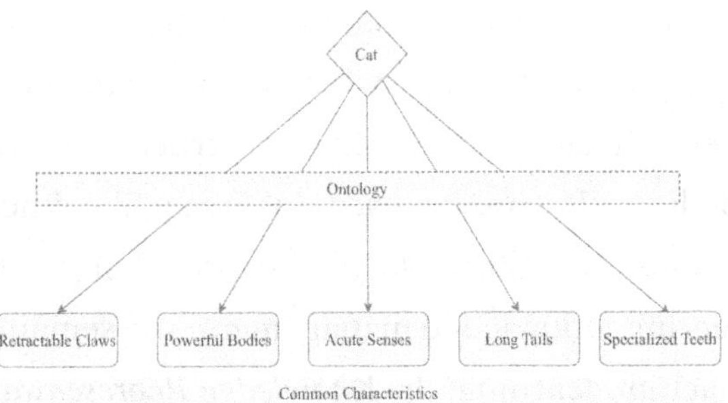

Figure 4.2: Ontology Knowledge Representation Example

it should focus on the traits of cats in general and capture traits that most cats might have. By doing this, use the ontology to explain more cats in the future. Figure 4.2 shows how ontology information can be represented. Ontologies work well with reasoning tools that can be used to draw new conclusions from a set of rules. Using logic can create a structured knowledge base that can't be wrong and can be queried for even the most complicated relationships. They are essential for sharing knowledge and *Semantic Web* application.

4.3.16 Handling Complex Knowledge: Hybrid Systems

Hybrid Systems typically employ more than one type of logic to solve complex problems in AI. For instance, learned embeddings can be added to knowledge graphs to make them better at answering questions and making decisions. A *Knowledge Graph* is a list of entities and the relationships between them. Getting knowledge graphs from Ontologies based on specific classes and traits is possible. A hybrid system also uses propositional logic (Cf. Chapter 4) for fundamental reasoning and fuzzy logic (Cf. Section 4.3.12) for dealing with uncertainty-related problems.

4.4 Summary

Propositional logic is an important and useful tool in AI, and this chapter explains it. Moreover, it is simple, accurate, and perfect for representing structured information and reasoning. Propositions, logical operators, and reasoning rules are used, and propositional logic lets AI systems model, conclude, and make intelligent choices in various situations. But, as we've seen in this chapter, propositional reasoning has some drawbacks. It also needs help dealing with uncertainty, the need for expressiveness in complex real-world information, and the fact that some AI domains are constantly changing. AI has developed new ways to deal with these problems, such as probabilistic logic, fuzzy logic, predicate logic, Ontologies, and hybrid systems, which we discussed in this chapter. These methods give AI more freedom in representing information and making decisions. Propositional logic is too easy for some AI model optimizations as a whole. Therefore, these ideas from propositional logic can be used in predicate logic, which will be discussed in the chapter 5.

4.4.1   Multiple Choice Questions

Exercise 1: Which of these is a combination of atomic proposition?

a) Continuous proposition

b) Compound proposition

c) Atomic proposition

d) Negation

Exercise 2: Which assigns the truth of any proposition statement?

a) Fuzzy logic   b) Hybrid system

c) Propositional   logic   d) Ontologies
   semantics

Exercise 3: Which of these is the negation symbol?

a) $\wedge$ b) $\vee$

c) $\neg$ d) $\rightarrow$

Exercise 4: A proposition is true under all cases in the last column of its truth table is called

a) Contradiction   b) Tautology

c) Atomic proposition   d) Compound
                                proposition

Exercise 5: A proposition is false under all cases in the last column of its truth table is called

a) Contradiction   b) Tautology

c) Atomic proposition   d) Compound
                                proposition

Exercise 6:   Which of the following holds for commutative property?

a) $P \wedge Q = Q \wedge P$ b) $(P \vee Q) \vee R = P \vee (Q \vee R)$

c) $(P \wedge Q) \wedge R = P \wedge (Q \wedge R)$ d) $\neg \neg P$

Exercise 7: A hybrid system uses propositional logic for fundamental reasoning and fuzzy logic for dealing with uncertainty-related problems. State whether it is True or False.

a) True   b) False

4.4.2   Short Answer Type Questions

1. Define propositional logic and how it differs from fuzzy logic.

2. What are the issues of using propositional logic to describe the knowledge base?

3. Write a short note on description logic.

4. Write in English the negation of each statement.
   (a) If I had 1,000,000 rupees, I'd buy you a car.
   (b) If it is not windy, I will go cycling.
   (c) A day that's cold and too windy is not a good day for walking on the street.

5. What is ontology in knowledge representation, and how does it differ from knowledge graph?

4.4.3　Long Answer Type Questions

1. Show that $(P{\rightarrow}Q){\leftrightarrow}(Q{\rightarrow}P)$ is neither a tautology nor a contradiction.

2. Show that $(P{\rightarrow}Q){\rightarrow}[(P{\rightarrow}Q){\rightarrow}Q]$ is a tautology. If not, what is the reason?

3. Show that the two statements $(P{\wedge}Q){\rightarrow}R$ and $(P{\rightarrow}R){\wedge}(Q{\rightarrow}R)$ are not logically equivalent.

4. Draw a syntax tree for the statement $\neg((\neg P{\wedge}Q){\vee}R)$.

5. Discuss the operator's properties in propositional logic with suitable examples.

Chapter 5

Predicate Logic

5.1 Goal of the Chapter

The prior chapter 4 discussed the AI model for representing knowledge using propositional logic. Therefore, this propositional logic is too easy and only works with simple sentences. However, a method known as predicate logic can help fix these kinds of issues. Predicate logic is strong enough to handle any sentence that is usually hard to understand. Consequently, this chapter explains the basic mathematical ideas behind predicate logic. Later, it goes into more depth about the syntax of AI predicate logic and its main components. Additionally, this chapter shows the different kinds of quantifiers and their features. This part ends with discussing forward chaining, backward chaining, and resolution.

5.2   Introduction

A formal logic used in AI called *Predicate Logic* is also known as *First-Order* or *First-Order Predicate Logic.* It shows facts, sentences, and the complicated relationships between them. It's used to show how a sentence is put together and how entities relate to each other. Another thing is that predicates are functions that connect variables to truth values, which are either true or false. "Rohit is a Champion"∧"Kohli is a Champion"∧"Sachin is a Champion" is an example. Then, make a template that has the Champion function.   So, the words "Champion(Rohit)"∧"Champion(Kohli)"∧"Champion(Sachin)" are now true. Champion() is one of these functions and is called a predicate.   Logical connective AND(∧) is used to connect all the sentences correctly, which helps to figure out the predicates.   Back in the 1950s and 1960s, predicate logic was first used in computers to make systems that could solve complex problems.   It was used to make *Prolog,* a first-order programming language that used logical rules and heuristics to help computers answer problems [Kow74]. Knowledge representation is the study of how to show information in a way that computers or people can use to reason with predicates and solve complex problems. Predicate logic is an integral part of this field. To help you understand predicate logic like this: In propositional logic, fundamental propositions can be broken down further using predicates, qualities given to subjects. This is what predicate logic is all about. To see this more clearly, let's say that "Delhi is the capital of India."We can show Delhi with the lowercase letter "d" and the claim that Delhi is the capital of India with an uppercase letter, say "C." We get "d is C." *Quantifiers* are used in predicate logic to show how far the predicate goes over the subject term. A quantifier needs to make more sense since Delhi is a single object in the first example. Let us retake the wolf example; the subject term is the idea of wolves in general, so write it as W and cute as C. We write "All W is C" because the sentence says all wolves are soft. This is how the matter is put in the usual *Aristotelian* way [Mal13]. But in present predicate logic, the quantifier is shown by one of these two signs, such as the universal quantifier $\forall$ means "all" or "every," and the existential quantifier $\exists$ means "some" or "there exists". Then, this quantifier is used on a group of things, shown by lowercase letters like x or y. To say that all wolves are cute, we can say that all wolves are cute, or even better, all things that are anything are cute if they are wolves. We can write like

$$\forall\!\forall_x (W_x \Rightarrow\Rightarrow C_x)$$

So, unlike propositional logic, predicate logic can deal with groups of entities, which makes it very useful in AI.

5.3   Fundamentals

In AI, predicate logic doesn't just include facts like propositional logic does; it also includes objects, relations, and functions. Objects can be anything in the real world or a variable, like colors, shapes, P, Q, etc. Then, relationships show how two objects are connected. It can make it a unary or n-array. A unary array defines the relations in a single term, while an n-array defines the relationships between n-terms. Blue and earth are examples of a unary array, whereas friends and brothers are examples of an n-array. One of the most essential things in predicate logic is the function. Functions like champion() (Cf. Section 5.2), father(), mother-of(), and more use their underlying relation to map their input object to their output object. With *Predicates*, *Variables*, and *Quantifiers*, predicate logic is usually used to write complicated expressions in simpler ways. In propositional logic, the facts of the natural world can be easily shown as well-formed formulas for local statements. Let's look at a simple case to understand predicate logic better. Let's say that the statement "All green birds are beautiful". Now, specify the predicates. IsGreen(x): Defines the property that x is green. IsBeautiful(x): Defines the property that x is beautiful. Here is the expression that will be used for the statement.

$$\forall_x(\text{IsGreen}(x) \rightarrow \text{IsBeautiful}(x))$$

"For all x, if x is green, then x is beautiful." This is what the statement $\forall_x(\text{IsGreen}(x) \rightarrow \text{IsBeautiful}(x))$ means. The universal quantifier ($\forall$) tells us that the statement is true for all things in the domain: birds. The implication ($\rightarrow$) is used to connect the properties such as "IsGreen(x)" and "IsBeautiful(x)," which says if an object x is green, then it is also beautiful. The parts of predicate logic that will be discussed next are *Syntax* (Cf. Section 5.4) and *Semantics* (Cf. Section 5.5).

5.4   Predicate Logic Syntax

In AI, predicate logic has a well-defined syntax comprising *Terms*, *Predicates*, and *Logical Connectives*. To put it another way, the syntax of predicate logic, which is a set of symbols, is a logical statement. This syntax is used in predicate logic to write and understand complex formulas. It starts with well-defined syntax terms, the basic building blocks of predicate logic that stand for objects or values. There are three kinds of it: *Functions*, *Variables*, and *Constants*. In discourse, variables are signs that stand for values or objects. It is usually shown by letters like P, Q, R, etc. Constants are specific, constant objects in the domain that are usually indicated by words or symbols, like "Wolf," "Delhi," "Tamilnadu," and so on. Functions take in one or more terms and give back a new term. Functions are usually shown by names or symbols, like $sqrt()$, $f(x)$, etc. Predicates are statements that describe properties or relationships of things. They are the second well-defined syntax. Usually, predicate symbols and terms are used as inputs to build it. "IsGreen(x)" means that "x is green," and "IsParent(Alice, Bob)" means that "Alice is the parent of Bob." Finally, logical connectives are used to make complicated formulas by linking predicates or other logical formulas. The section 4.3.3 briefly explains the basics of logical connectives. Let's look at some simple examples of how logical connectives are used in predicate logic to help you understand them better. Start with the conjunction that looks like the symbol AND($\land$). "IsGreen(x) $\land$IsBeautiful(x)" means "x is green and x is beautiful." Then, there is a disjunction, shown by the OR($\lor$) sign. In this case, "IsGreen(x)$\lor$IsBeautiful(x)" means that "x is either green or beautiful." Negation is another logical link that stands for the symbol NOT($\neg$). This means that "$\neg$IsGreen(x)" means that "x is not green." The implication is that it stands for the IF, THEN($\rightarrow$) sign, which means that "IsGreen(x)$\rightarrow$IsBeautiful(x)" means "if x is green, then x is beautiful". Lastly, the biconditional sign stands for IF AND ONLY IF($\leftrightarrow$). "IsGreen(x,y) $\leftrightarrow$IsBeautiful(x,y)" means "x is green to y if and only if x is beautiful of y."

5.5 Predicate Logic Semantics

In AI, *Semantics* is all about the strategies used to evaluate a statement of *Predicate Logic*. These methods use several known relationships and facts about the world to figure out the boolean value of a given predicate logic expression. To clarify things, the semantics of predicate logic tell us if a formula or statement is true or false. Based on how the predicate symbols, constants, variables, and logical connectives are interpreted, the truth value of a formula is found. It starts with interpretation and sets the domain of a set of objects. It also gives constant meanings and describes the relationships that predicates define. In an explanation, "Bob" could mean a specific person, "IsBlue" could mean the sky, and "IsBeautiful" could mean a person. Atomic formulas are another way to evaluate statements. Atomic formulas are checked by replacing the constants or variables with the values given to them in the interpretation. The atomic formula is true if the predicate holds for the specific objects and how they relate. If not, it is false. The evaluation of complex formulas is the third type of evaluation in the semantics of predicate logic. Truth tables are used to evaluate complex formulas related to propositional logic (Cf. Section 4.3.4). There are logical connectives that determine the truth value of compound sentences by looking at the truth values of the formulas that make them up. IsDog(x)∧IsBarking(x) is true if both "IsDog(x)" and "IsBarking(x)" are true. The predicate syntax comprises terms, atomic formulas, and logical connectives that work together to make complicated statements. In predicate logic, the semantics involve:

- Figuring out what these statements mean in a particular environment.

- Giving them true values based on the meanings of symbols and logical connectives.

- Deciding if a formula is true or false in that environment.

This is the basis for the fundamental reasoning skills in both AI and formal logic.

5.6   Predicate Logic Basic Elements

Predicate logic requires basic elements to achieve its objectives. Constants, variables, predicates, *Equality*, function, quantifiers, connectives, and more are some of the most essential elements of predicate logic. Take a look at the predicates. These are statements that can be true or false based on the reasons given for them. They show the properties and relationships of their objects. "IsBarking(x)" is an example of a predicate. "x" is a variable that stands for an object, and the predicate is true if the object is barking. Variables are another essential element. They are made up of symbols that can have different values. Variables in predicate logic stand for things in the domain of discourse, which is a set of objects. "x" in "IsBarking(x)" can stand for any item in the domain, like a *German Shepherd*, *Poodle*, or *Beagle*. Subsequently, a constant is a number that doesn't change. They stand for particular objects in the domain. In knowledge of context information, for example, "Thiruvarur is in Tamilnadu" could be a constant that stands for a specific place. In logical representations, quantifiers are also used to define the range of values. Existential and universal quantifiers are the two main quantifiers in predicate logic. Using the existential quantifier $\exists$ means that there is at least one object for which the statement inside the quantifier

Table 5.1: Basic Elements of Predicate Logic

Element	Sample	Purpose
Connectives	$\wedge, \vee, \neg, \rightarrow, \rightleftharpoons$	Used to construct complex sentences
Constant	India,Bird,Y,4	Nothing can be changed about these values
Equality	$==$	Used to checks equality
Function	sqrt()	Finds a specific relation of an input term
Predicates	Father, Mother $<$	Establishes a relation between in its terms
Quantifier	$\forall, \exists$	Assesses a quantity on the individual variable
Variables	p,q,r,m,n	Can change and take on any value

is true. One example is "$\exists x$ IsBarking(x)," which says that at least one object is barking. When you see the symbol $\forall$ for a universal quantifier, the statement inside is true for all objects in the domain. As an example, "$\forall x$ IsCar(x)$\rightarrow$IsWheel(x)" says that all cars have wheels. In predicate logic, these elements make up the syntax, which lets us make explicit declarations about objects and their properties in a formal and organized way. The basic elements of predicate logic in AI can be seen in Table 5.1.

5.7 Atomic Sentences

The most basic statements in AI's predicate logic are *Atomic Sentences*. One predicate and a group of terms

enclosed in parentheses make up these sentences. To put
it more formally, the framework of an atomic sentence
looks like this:

$$\text{Predicate (term}_1\text{, term}_2\text{, term}_3 \ldots \text{term}_n)$$

Table 5.2: Examples of Atomic Sentences in Predicate
Logic

Atomic Sentences	Predicates
Kohli and Rohit are friends	Friends (Kohli, Rohit)
American Shorthair is a cat	Cat (American Shorthair)
Yousuf and Irfan are brothers	Brothers (Yousuf, Irfan)
German Shepherd is a dog	Dog (German Shepherd)
Square is a rhombus	Rhombus (Square)
Dingo is a wolf	Wolf (Dingo)
Circle is a curve	Curve (Circle)
Mary-Kate and Ashley Olsen are sisters	Sisters (Mary-Kate, Ashley Olsen)
Toucan is a Neotropical bird	Bird (Toucan)

The examples of atomic statements in predicate logic are
shown in Table 5.2.

5.8   Complex Sentences

Logical connectives like AND ($\wedge$), OR ($\vee$), NOT ($\neg$),
IMPLIES ($\rightarrow$), and more are used to put together atomic

sentences to make *Complex Sentences.* If m_1, m_2... m_n are connectives, then describe a complex sentence in AI predicate logic:

$$\text{Predicate}_1(\text{term}_1, \text{term}_2,\ldots)m_1 \; \text{Predicate}_2(\text{term}_1, \text{term}_2,\ldots)m_2 \ldots \text{Predicate}_n (\text{term}_1, \text{term}_2,\ldots)m_n$$

Table 5.3: Examples of Complex Sentences in Predicate Logic

S.No	Predicates: Complex Sentences
1	Friends (Kohli, Rohit) $\wedge$ Friends (Rohit, Kohli)
2	Brothers (Yousuf, Irfan) $\wedge$ Brothers (Irfan, Yousuf)
3	Cat (American Shorthair) $\vee$ Cat (Siamese)
4	Dog (German Shepherd) $\rightarrow$ $\neg$Dog(Australian Shepherd)

Table 5.3 shows an example of complex sentences in AI predicate logic. Any statement in predicate logic can also be broken down into two parts: the subject and the predicate. The subject is usually the main thing that the phrase talks about. However, a predicate is a relationship connecting two basic statements. "Z is a whole number" is an example of a statement. It has two parts: "Z" is the subject, and "is a whole number" is the predicate. It's necessary to measure everything in the environment

once make complex sentences. *Quantifiers* are used to do this, which will be covered in the next Section 5.9.

5.9   Quantifiers

Describing statements in predicate logic without using a specific constant symbol through quantification is possible. As the word "quantifier" means, they are used to rate the importance of the environment in an AI system. Figuring out how many specific entities are in the environment and meeting a particular condition "counts" in AI. The range and scope of a variable in a logical statement can also be found using quantifiers. Universal and existential quantifiers are the two main quantifiers discussed in Section 5.9.1 and 5.9.2.

5.9.1   Universal Quantifier

A *Universal Quantifier* is used when all class elements have the same attribute. It says a statement is true for all objects in the discourse domain. The "upside-down A" ($\forall$) in formal logic shows the universal quantifier. It means "All," which is a Quantifier since "All" is the number that includes everything in a given environment.

$\forall_z$ means "For all z," or "For every z," or "For each z" if "z" is a variable. Table 5.4 shows an example of a universal quantifier, which shows sentences and their logical notations. As an example, with the table as a

Table 5.4: A Typical Example of Universal Quantifier

Statements	Logical Notations
Every student likes vacation	$\forall_z$ Student(z) $\rightarrow$ likes(z, Vacation)
Everyone likes burger	$\forall_x$ Everyone(x) $\rightarrow$ likes(x, Burger)
Everyone likes cricket	$\forall_y$ Everyone(y) $\rightarrow$ likes(y, Cricket)
All humans need oxygen to live	$\forall_x$
All is well	$\forall_y$

guide, the sentence "Every Student Likes Vacation" can be written as $\forall_z$ Student(z) $\rightarrow$ likes(z, Vacation). This could mean there is every z, where 'z' is a student who likes vacation. In the same way, all of the statements can be put in this way.

5.9.2 Existential Quantifier

An *Existential Quantifier* means that the statement they apply to is true for at least one case of something. The symbol for this in formal logic is the "backward E"($\exists$). This phrase means "there is at least one" or "there exists." Additionally, the sign for "AND($\wedge$)" is always required. Formal logic uses these symbols to make writing sentences faster so that they focus on the logic instead of the statement itself. If 'y' is variable, for instance, $\exists_y$ means "For some y," or "There exists an y," or "For at least one y." Let's take the "trees" and use the letter "x" to represent "trees." This formal writing can say, "There exists at least one tree that produces mangos." Included in the Table 5.5 are sentences and their

Table 5.5: An Example of Existential Quantifier

Statements	Logical Notations
Some student likes vacation	$\exists_y$: Student(y)$\wedge$likes Vacation(y)
Some people likes burger	$\exists_z$: People(z)$\wedge$likes Burger(z)
Some people likes cricket	$\exists_x$: People(x)$\wedge$likes Cricket(x)
There exists at least one active subscription	$\exists_x$
There exists at least one outlier in the data set	$\exists_z$

logical notations that show an example of an existential quantifier. The sentence "Some Student Likes Vacation" from the Table 5.5 can be written in logical notation as "$\exists_y$: Student(y)$\wedge$likes Vacation(y)". The meaning of this could be: There is some 'y' where y is a student who likes vacation. Similarly, all of the statements can be put in the same way.

5.9.3   Nested Quantifier

One or more quantifiers can be nested inside another quantifier, making *Nested Quantifiers* propositional functions. There are four different ways that they can be nested. With the $\exists_m \forall_n$ symbols, these quantifiers can be shown. As in $\forall_m \exists_n (mn = 0)$, two quantifiers are nested if one covers the other. In this case, $\forall_m Q(m)$ means the same thing as $\exists_n P(m, n)$, where $P(m, n)$ means $mn = 0$. For instance, let's say that all real numbers make up the scope for the variables 'm' and 'n'. All real numbers 'm' and 'n' are equal, as shown by the statement $\forall_m \forall_n (mn = nm)$. To add real numbers, they must follow this rule. For

Table 5.6:   An Example of Quantifications of Two Variables

Quantifications	Statements
$\forall_m \forall_n P(m,n)$	Everyone likes everybody
$\forall_m \exists_n P(m,n)$	Everyone likes someone
$\exists_m \forall_n P(m,n)$	Someone likes everyone
$\exists_m \exists_n P(m,n)$	Someone likes somebody
$\forall_n \forall_m P(m,n)$	Everybody is likes by everyone
$\forall_n \exists_m P(m,n)$	Everyone is liked by someone
$\exists_n \forall_m P(m,n)$	There is someone whom everyone likes
$\exists_n \exists_m P(m,n)$	There is someone whom someone likes

the same reason, the statement $\forall_m \exists_n (mn = 0)$ means that there is a real number 'n' such that mn=0 for every real number 'm'. Every real number has an opposite, which is a multiple of itself. A similar rule applies to multiplying real numbers: $\forall_m \forall_n \forall_o (m(no)) = ((mn) o)$ (Cf. Section 4.3.8). Another thing to remember is that the order of the quantifiers matters unless they are all existential or universal. Two quantifiers can be used with two variables in eight different ways: $\forall_m \forall_n$, $\forall_m \exists_n$, $\exists_m \forall_n$, $\exists_m \exists_n$, $\forall_n \forall_m$, $\forall_n \exists_m$, $\exists_n \forall_m$, $\exists_n \exists_m$. Table 5.6 shows an example of quantifying two variables and what it means if $P(m, n) = $ m likes n.

5.10   Inference Rules

Inference is the process of making new sentences out of old ones. *Inference Rules*, conversely, are used to create new logical sentences out of logical sentences that have already been proven. The structures of those sentences are like specific formal language structures, like formulas or sequences. In this case, seeing a father slap his son makes you infer that the son did something wrong—a set of premises and a conclusion make up an inference rule. Predicate logic is a set of inference rules for drawing conclusions from other sets of inference rules, or it can be used by itself. It is said that an argument is valid when the result is true when all the beliefs are true. On the other hand, an argument is false when none of the beliefs are true. The next part discusses Modus Ponens 5.10.1 and Universal Instantiation 5.10.2, two important inference rules in predicate logic.

5.10.1   Modus Ponens

Modus Ponens is a way to draw a conclusion from logical inference. This simple rule about what "if" means in logic. It can conclude a conditional sentence and the part that comes before it is called the "if" part. This is how the rule can be written: If a conditional statement like "If A, then B" $(A{\rightarrow}B)$ is true and that A is true, then B must also be true. This is because a conditional can only be true when both the antecedent and the conclusion are true. Also, "if" means "if A is false, then B is false." In the first part, all the possible outcomes were named. After that, the second part concludes which case fits: A is true. Since they already said what consequence goes with "A" being true, all they have to do is say the result that goes with that claim. Modus ponens can be used on both propositional and predicate forms in predicate logic. In this case, if you have the following condition formulas:

$$\text{IsThirst}(x) \rightarrow \text{WillDrink}(x)$$
$$\text{IsThirst}(\text{Alice})$$

From the sentences, use modus ponens to figure out that "WillDrink(Alice)" is true since "IsThirst(Alice)" is true. In the same way, let's conclude "Pigs can fly" based on the statements "The moon is blue" and "If the moon is blue, then pigs can fly." The important thing about modus ponens is that it shows the other half of what implication means: the removal half. The introduction of implication is the other half of the meaning of implication. This idea is sometimes known as the rule of implication. This is how it goes. In the end, they can conclude $A \rightarrow B$ if, after assuming statement A, they can figure out statement B. Modus ponens is an elementary and precise idea, but *Lewis Carroll* enjoyed it in his story "What the Tortoise Said to Achilles [Car18]."

5.10.2   Universal Instantiation

The *Universal Instantiation* inference rule works with statements universally quantified ($\forall$) in predicate logic. It lets us draw conclusions about specific cases by replacing the universally quantified variables with constants. In this way, the rule can be stated: assume if you have a universally quantified statement like " $\forall_z P(z)$ " that means $P(z)$ is true for all 'z', you can make it true for a particular value by replacing "z" with that value. This lets you conclude that $P(c)$ is true for any constant 'c' in a set of conversation. An example of universal instantiation is illustrated in Table 5.7. Let's look at a simple example

Table 5.7: An Example of Universal Instantiation

Universal Quantifications	Universal Statements
$\forall_z$ IsHuman(z) $\rightarrow$ IsOxygen(z)	All humans need oxygen to live
$\forall_x$ IsDog(x) $\rightarrow$ IsMammal(x)	All dogs are mammals
$\forall_y$ IsHuman(y) $\rightarrow$ IsMammal(y)	All humans are mammals
$\forall_y$ IsHuman(y) $\rightarrow$ IsMortal(y)	All humans are mortal
$\forall_x$ IsBlood(x) $\rightarrow$ IsRed(x)	All blood is red

of how universal instantiation works. Figure out which statement from the Table 5.7 is the universally quantified one: " $\forall_z$ IsHuman(z) $\rightarrow$ IsOxygen(z)," which means "All humans need oxygen to live." Because "IsHuman(Alice)" is true, you can use Universal Instantiation to figure out that "IsOxygen(Alice)" is true for a specific person in the domain named "Alice." In the same way, the universally quantified statement "$\forall_x$ IsDog(x) $\rightarrow$ IsMammal(x)" says, "All dogs are mammals." We can see that "IsMammal(Poppy)" is true for a specific dog in the domain named "Poppy" because "IsDog(Poppy)" is true. In predicate logic, modus ponens and universal instantiation rules are essential to logical reasoning. They help to draw a proper conclusion from the provided rules and premises. In AI, for an intelligent agent to make good choices and act quickly, it must know about the real world. The knowledge base and the inference engine are usually its two main parts. In the *Knowledge Base*, there is a list of sentences, and it is also a technical term that is different from English. Meanwhile, the *Inference Engine* uses logical rules like backward and forward chaining to get new information from the knowledge base. Thus, discuss these rules in Sections 5.11 and 5.12.

5.11 Solution: Forward Chaining

Forward Chaining is a way for AI to assess and solve problems. It's also known as an *Inference Engine, Forward Deduction,* or *Forward Thinking.* Forward chaining is a part of the *Expert System* that uses the knowledge base and reasoning rules to discover new information. To find answers, it looks at the facts in the knowledge base and figures out what they mean. AI uses this way of reasoning to start with atomic phrases in the knowledge base and then uses inference rules to get new data until the goal is met. It is noted that the facts are known, so the inference rule is applied whose premises are met. Then, the new data drawn from the facts is added to the known facts, and the process is repeated until the goal is reached. The inference engine's main thing is going through the inference rules until it finds one where the antecedent or if clause is indeed true. Once the inference engine finds a rule that fits, it can determine what will happen next, i.e., the then clause. These lead to adding new data, and the inference engine keeps doing this repeatedly until it gets to its goal. Figure 5.1 shows a typical case of forward chaining. Undoubtedly, forward chaining chooses which rule to apply based on the environment. If there are a thousand or more rules, the simple check would be to go through each one repeatedly whenever something changes. The big step ahead in forward chaining began as a PhD thesis at Carnegie Mellon University in the late 1970s [For79]. Afterward, Forgy and Charles devised a quick way to solve the problem of matching many

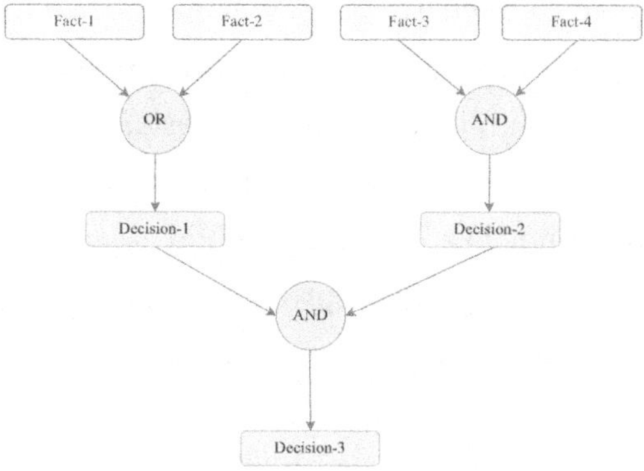

Figure 5.1: A Standard Example of Forward Chaining

patterns and objects [For89]. As they work toward their goal, like making moves in a chess game, they look at the set of rules and devise a quick way to check only the rules that a change in the state might change. It is like this is what made expert systems possible. In the forward-chaining method, a set of known data is given to the researcher or machine. Then, they use this data to do the necessary calculations and come to a conclusion. It is the journey from the initial state to the goal state, simply. For example, let's say Kumar works as a lecturer. He is given the grades his students got on different projects, tasks, and internal tests. He has to develop a mathematical model to tell which students will pass or fail the final exams. In this case, he already has the available data, which includes grades from regular tests, homework, and projects. He must conclude whether the student will pass or fail the final exam. This method is also known as the "top-down approach," primarily used for planning, designing, interpreting, drawing conclusions, and other similar tasks. In this case, the study might begin with a few initial states and end with many conclusions. There may be an infinite number of possible decisions at times. Also, this method might try to figure out many things from the input data, but not all have to be part of the goal state. The main problems with forward chaining are that it takes time and the facts are unclear. These issues can be fixed with backward chaining, which will be discussed in the next Section 5.12.

5.12   Solution: Backward Chaining

The *Backward Chaining* method starts with the goal and works backward, using rules to find known facts to help the goal. This type of method is also known as *Backward Deduction* or *Backward Reasoning* when an inference engine is used. The goal is known to the inference engine in this case. The method then starts with the goal and works backward to determine what facts must be said to reach the goal. There is also a start with the conclusion, which is then supported by a list of facts. Going from the top to the bottom is how up-down chaining works. In the backward chaining process, the *Modus Ponens* (Cf. Section 5.10.1) reasoning rule is what it all starts with. Smaller goals are within the main goal to show that the facts are correct. Because of this, it is called a goal-driven method because the rules are chosen and used based on a list of goals. Figure 5.2 shows a typical case of backward chaining. Let's discuss more information to help you

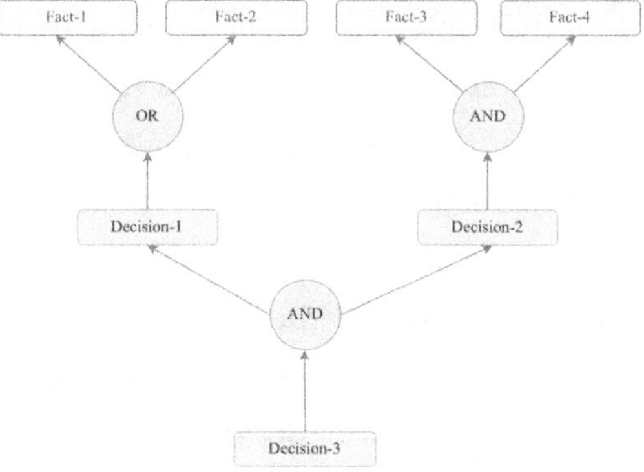

Figure 5.2: A Typical Example of Backward Chaining

understand backward chaining better. In this method, the researcher or machine is given some inferences. It then uses these inferences to follow some inference rules and find the facts that lead to the inferences. In other words, it starts from the goal and goes to the initial state. For example, consider the case discussed before (Cf. Section 5.11) and consider Kumar, a lecturer. He has now been given the final examination results of a certain number of students and is not to worry about the results, whether they passed or failed. Now, Kumar has to look into it and determine what caused a student to pass or fail the final examination. After much research and math, he may have found the following facts: Students who got more than 70% on their internal examinations usually do well on their final exams and pass. Many students who got less than 40% on their internal tests also fail their final exams. Most students who got more than 80% on their assignments pass the final exams, while most students who got less than 50% fail the exams. The information above shows that the internal tests and assignments were essential in preparing students for the final exams and determining their scores. This method is also known as the goal-driven or bottom-up approach, and it's primarily used for fixing bugs, diagnoses, treatment strategies, and other similar tasks. The study might begin in a few goal states and end up in many starting states. From a historical point of view, there will not be an endless number of initial states or facts. This method might find the essential facts for the goal. So, there is a smaller chance that it tries to answer questions outside its current scope. The main problem with the backward chaining method is that it must know the goal state before moving on to the initial states. But sometimes, the facts need to be clarified. So, there needs to be a way to show that sentences or facts are satisfiable automatically. These problems can be solved with resolution, which will be discussed in the next section 5.13.

5.13   Theorem Proving: Resolution

Resolution is a robust inference rule and one of the most essential ideas in propositional logic for logical reasoning. It is a method for automatically proving theorems, storing information, and drawing conclusions from existing propositional logic knowledge bases. The resolution rule is a vital part of resolution-based theorem-proving. It is based on the rules of logical reasoning.

There needs to be proof of the conclusion of the claims if more than one is given. To resolve a problem, we generally use the proof-of-contradiction principle. In propositional and predicate logic, a knowledge base is usually shown as a group of clauses, where each clause is a list of literals that don't belong together. We get a literal if we remove a propositional variable (P, Q, R, etc.). If we remove a propositional variable, we get a literal. It should contradict the conclusion to find the conclusion. Then, the resolution rule is used on the terms that are left over. Each clause with literals that go with each other is resolved to make two new clauses that can be added to the facts. If it's not already there, that is written down. This process continues until two things happen: no more clauses can be added, or the resolution rule is used to get the empty clause. If there is an empty clause, it means that the negation of the conclusion is a complete contradiction. This means that either the negation of the conclusion is invalid or false, or the assertion is valid. If one of two atomic propositions in an OR($\vee$) proposition is false, the other must be true. This is what the resolution inference rule says. Let's look at an example: If we know that either "Rohit is in the cricket ground" or "Kohli is in the dressing room," we can also say that "Rohit is not in the cricket ground." This means that "Kohli is in the dressing room." To be more authorized, we can say the following about the resolution: Before using resolution, we must turn the knowledge base into a list of phrases. Each sentence tells something or follows a rule. The resolution rule is based on the idea that we can eliminate redundant literals if we join two clauses with complimentary literals. To give an

Table 5.8: An Example of Propositional Resolution

Step	Rule	Inference
1	P ∨ Q	Stated
2	¬P ∨ R	Stated
3	¬Q ∨ R	Stated
4	¬R	Negated Conclusion
5	Q ∨ R	1,2[(P∨Q)∨(¬P∨R)]
6	¬P	2,4[(¬P∨R)∨(¬R)]
7	¬Q	3,4[(¬Q∨R)∨(¬R)]
8	R	5,7[(Q∨R)∨(¬Q)]
9	□	4,8[(¬R)∨(R)]

example, if we have the clauses (P∨Q) and (P→R), we can get rid of P to get the new clause (Q∨R). By applying the resolution rule over and over to the knowledge base's clauses, we can find new clauses that weren't stated directly but make sense based on what is already known. This process lets you draw conclusions and inferences based on the data stored in the propositional logic and predicate knowledge bases. Let's look at another example to help you understand closure better. Assume that we know both "Rohit is in the cricket ground" and "Kohli is in the dressing room." We also know "Rohit is not in the cricket ground" and "Sachin is eating." Using resolution, we can determine that "Kohli is in the dressing room" OR($\vee$) "Sachin is eating." To use proper phrasing: When we use complementary literals, we can make new words by concluding them. In this way, inference rules find compatible literals to create new knowledge. Let's use the following phrases in Table 5.8 to show that "R is false": $P \vee Q$, $P \rightarrow R$, and $Q \rightarrow R$. Now, resolve lines 1 and 2 and get "$Q \vee R$" by removing P. Next, we can eliminate R in lines 2 and 4 to get "$\neg P$." In the same way, we can get "$\neg Q$" by removing R from lines 3 and 4. We get R by getting rid of Q in lines 5 and 7. Finally, we get the false, empty clause when we remove R from lines 4 and 8. This little box often shows that we've gotten the desired contradiction (Cf. Section 4.3.6). We can also select any order for a given rule. Overall, resolution is a robust tool for AI systems that do automated reasoning, prove theorems, and solve hard logical problems by methodically getting new information from rules and propositions that are already known.

5.14   Summary

This chapter introduces predicate logic, an essential way to represent information and reason, an important part of artificial intelligence. It lets us describe and quantify complex relationships in a helpful way in many AI applications, ranging from knowledge representation to automated reasoning, which this chapter talks about. Even though it has problems and restrictions, predicate logic makes it possible to create intelligent systems that can understand and communicate with the world in a structured and logical way, which is what this chapter was about. This chapter concludes that predictive logic can help AI systems become more intelligent and capable, moving the field forward and constructing new opportunities for future uses.

5.14.1 Multiple Choice Questions

Exercise 1: Which of the following connects the complex sentences?

a) Constant   b) Connectives c) Function   d) Variables

Exercise 2: Which one of the following cannot change values?

a) Constant   b) Connectives c) Function   d) Variables

Exercise 3: Which of the following is a complex sentence in predicate logic?

a) Friends (Kohli, Rohit)

b) Sisters (Mary-Kate, Ashley Olsen)

c) Brothers (Yousuf, Irfan)

d) Friends (Kohli, Rohit) ∧ Friends (Rohit, Kohli)

Exercise 4: Which of the following does not belong to atomic sentences in predicate logic?

a) Brothers (Yousuf, Irfan)

b) Friends (Kohli, Rohit) ∧ Friends (Rohit, Kohli)

c) Friends (Kohli, Rohit)

d) Sisters (Mary-Kate, Ashley Olsen)

Exercise 5: What is the correct logical notation of the following statement into a universal quantifier? "Every student likes vacation"

a) $\forall_z$ Student(z) $\rightarrow$ likes(z, Vacation)

b) $\forall_x$ Everyone(x) $\rightarrow$ likes(x, Burger)

c) $\forall_y$ Everyone(y) $\rightarrow$ likes(y, Cricket)

d) $\forall_x$

Exercise 6: What is the correct logical notation of the following statement into a universal quantifier? "Everyone likes cricket"

a) $\forall_y$ Everyone(y) $\rightarrow$ likes(y, Cricket)

b) $\forall_x$

c) $\forall_z$ Student(z) $\rightarrow$ likes(z, Vacation)

d) $\forall_x$ Everyone(x) $\rightarrow$ likes(x, Burger)

Exercise 7: What is the correct logical notation of the following statement into an existential quantifier? "Some student likes vacation"

a) $\exists_y$: Student(y)$\wedge$likes Vacation(y)

b) $\exists_z$

c) $\exists_x$: People(x)∧likes Cricket(x)

d) $\exists_z$: People(z)∧likes Burger(z)

Exercise 8: What is the correct logical notation of the following statement into an existential quantifier? "Some people likes cricket"

a) $\exists_x$: People(x)∧likes Cricket(x)

b) $\exists_z$: People(z)∧likes Burger(z)

c) $\exists_y$: Student(y)∧likes Vacation(y)

d) $\exists_z$

Exercise 9: What is predicate logic's correct universal statement of the following universal quantification? "$\forall_z$ IsHuman(z) → IsOxygen(z)"

a) All dogs are mammals

b) All blood is red

c) All humans need oxygen to live

d) All humans are mortal

Exercise 10: What is predicate logic's correct universal statement of the following universal quantification? "$\forall_x$ IsDog(x) → IsMammal(x)"

a) All humans need oxygen to live

b) All humans are mortal

c) All dogs are mammals

d) All blood is red

Exercise 11: Which of these is not a kind of inference?

a) Backward Chaining

b) Modus Ponens

c) Resolution

d) Forward Chaining

Exercise 12: Forward chaining is a part of the Expert System that uses the knowledge base and reasoning rules to discover new information. State whether it is True or False.

a) True

b) False

5.14.2   Short Answer Type Questions

1. Why does artificial intelligence need predicate logic?

2. Define predicate logic and how it differs from propositional logic.

3. Represent atomic sentences and complex sentences.

4. Write short notes on Modus Ponens.

5. Write the following sentences in the form of predicates:
   (a) All the children like toys.
   (b) Someone likes everyone.
   (c) Everyone likes someone.
   (d) If everyone likes everyone, then someone likes someone.

5.14.3 Long Answer Type Questions

1. Demonstrate how predicate logic can be used to represent knowledge in AI.

2. Discuss the different types of quantifiers in propositional logic with suitable examples.

3. Explain forward-chaining and backward-chaining techniques with the help of an example.

4. I) Transform the following into predicates:
   a. Rohit travels by bus if available; otherwise travels by train.
   b. Train goes via Thanjavur and Tiruchirappalli.
   c. The bus has a puncture, so it is not available.

II) Will Rohit travel via Tiruchirappalli? Use forward chaining.

5. Briefly illustrate the fundamental working procedures of the Resolution inference rule with a suitable example.

Chapter 6

Optimization Algorithms

6.1 Goal of the Chapter

The previous chapter 5 discussed the AI model for representing knowledge using predicate logic. As a result, the predicate model performs better for most complicated sentences. However, AI-based optimization is complex and challenging to handle and improve in intricate systems. The main goal of AI-based optimization is to make the system work better and simplify. For this reason, this chapter introduces the basics of optimization in artificial intelligence. It also goes into depth about different optimization algorithms and the problems they face. Finally, this chapter talks about learning automata-based optimization algorithms and their challenges.

6.2   Introduction

Artificial Intelligence Optimization, or *AIO*, has tremendous potential for making intelligent decisions in today's information-based services. There is now one question: what is optimization? *Optimization* is all about an algorithm that tries to find the best solution to a problem out of all the ones that could work. Let me give you a simple example. If I give you three scoops of ice cream—one vanilla, one strawberry, and one chocolate—you enjoy picking the one you like best. When you go beyond this simple example, your choices change, and the way you measure worth changes, and there may be limits and uncertainties. These algorithms help people with complex environmental problems make the best choices in the real world. This saves time and resources and often leads to better results. A problem that must be solved to use an optimization method cannot exist. One or more optimization goals must be present, along with some limits or rules that our answer must follow. We need to know the optimization goal to make an optimization problem. That's the goal we want to reach. There don't have to be rules or limits for a problem to exist, but they generally do. These limits often make the optimization problem much more challenging to solve because they make it more complicated. Given the optimization problem, an optimization method is a way to find the best solution in a planned way. That expected outcome should also follow all the rules and limits for the optimization problem to be good. Most of the time, these involve solving models with many uncertain decision factors and parameters in many different ways and over many different time frames and scales. AIO is a method that blurs the lines between optimization and learning. This lets data shape the creation of better optimization algorithms that can learn and adjust to unique problems or fundamental issues in an application. At its core, optimization is about making plans and fixing problems. The best way to reach a specific goal or result is using structured data from techniques like *NLP* as context. The steps of the AI ladder are gathering, arranging, analyzing, infusing, and modernizing. These measures can improve AI usage. AI should be used to power databases to handle data more efficiently and quickly. For example, databases should be built to support AI and standard languages. We can optimize even more by using ML to improve how searches are run. The use of *Machine Learning* to enhance queries learns from how well they work and keeps improving the suggestions about the best way for queries to run. It works like a *Neural Network* to learn from experience in this way. Optimization looks like a lot of trial-and-error at its most basic level. The program changes how it works in small ways and checks to see if this gets it closer to its goal. But if it does, it keeps changing the way it acts. Something else is tried if that doesn't work. There are tens of thousands of optimization algorithms, each different. Some can only be used for specific problems and others for various issues. The following sections 6.3, 6.4, 6.5, 6.6, 6.7 talk about some of the most common optimization algorithms.

6.3 Deterministic Algorithms

The purpose of deterministic optimization is to find the global optimal solution. Theoretically, the outcome that is returned is always the global optimal solution. *Deterministic Optimization* algorithms do that by taking advantage of valuable parts of a problem. In deterministic optimization, the problem is set up so that the algorithm always finds the best solution for a particular set of inputs. For example, the pricing model is predictable if the position in the theater, the day of the month, and the time of the event are used to determine the ticket price. This is because the input given will always lead to the same price. There are no random or uncertain parts in the optimization process. The problem parameters and the optimization algorithm are the only things determining the solution. *Gradient Descent* is an example of a deterministic algorithm that is often used to find the best solution when the goal function is smooth and behaves well. Deterministic algorithms may need help with optimization functions that are very complicated and changeable. Still, these methods are often faster and can guarantee the best solution. This happens because the finding space is ample, and the problem structure is complicated. Several AI models can be used to create deterministic optimization algorithms [Flo13].

We can talk about some of them, like integer programming, non-convex nonlinear programming, mixed-integer nonlinear programming, structural programming, and more. It starts with *Linear Programming*, or LP, which is a mathematical model that models a problem and its requirements using linear relationships, which are relationships between two variables that are straight lines. It then uses linear objective functions to analyze the model. Another option is the *Non-Linear Programming Model* or NOLP model. Given the circumstances, there may be nonlinear connections between the problem, the constraints, and the objective functions. When it comes to deterministic optimization, these problems are challenging. The globally optimal solution is the best solution to a convex problem. Both LP and NOLP can be used to solve this problem. However, we have choices for non-convex optimization problems, which means many possible best solutions exist. Non-convex problems could be solved with *Integer Programming* or IP, *Non-Convex NonLinear*

Programming or NNLP, or *Mixed-Integer NonLinear Programming* or MINLP. Non-convex problems are used in discrete and continuous programming environments, which we discussed earlier in this Section 1.6. *Branch-and-Bound, Interval Analysis,* and more are some methods that can be used to perform deterministic optimization for these models. Ultimately, deterministic optimization methods are essential for using computers to solve problems. Deterministic optimization is necessary if the global optimal solution is to be achieved. It is usually better when the problem can be precisely modeled and the unknowns are small or can be ignored. Otherwise, it can't do what it's supposed to do in a given situation.

6.3.1   DSA: Problems to Address

There are three main categories of optimization algorithms: traditional, modern, and *No Free Lunch* theorem [Flo13], while an optimization problem has inputs, constraints, objectives, and components. The first step in solving an optimization problem is to identify its components. Input (decision variables), output (objective function), systems, and constraints are the standard building blocks of any optimization issue.

Assessing objective functions in the face of constraints is the fundamental goal of optimization issues. Possible outputs include the globally optimal solution to the current problem state, depending on the input variables and constraints. An illustration of how to formulate an optimization issue is shown in Figure 6.1. For the sake of argument, assume that we would like to design a table. Reducing the weight should be the primary goal. Similarly, length and width are inputs, while weight is

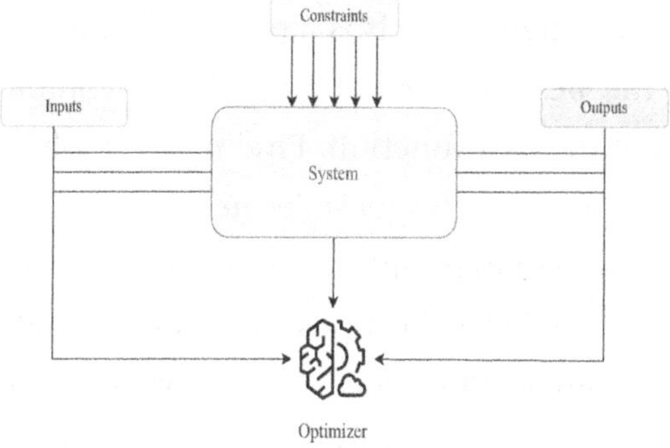

Figure 6.1: An Example of Formulate an Optimization Problem

an output. Subject to constraints such as 3 < length < 8 and 3 < width < 8, the objective functions are computed using the width and height. These are the steps for formulating optimization issues. An optimization method is employed to get the best possible outcome. The benefits of a deterministic optimization algorithm include a reduced number of function evaluations and a more reliable solution-seeking process. Nevertheless, several drawbacks exist, such as excessive reliance on the original solution, stagnation of local optima, the poor likelihood of discovering the global optimum, essential need gradient, and more. A deterministic algorithm might be best shown by the *Gradient Descent Optimization* algorithm. It is a popular ML technique for finding the best solution iteratively by computing the gradient of the cost function. Finding the global minima, where the error is the least, is its goal. It is also one of the most popular optimization algorithms in *Deep Learning*. Finding the best possible weights and biases is its primary goal. It provides a learning rate that dictates the size of the stages. Picking the correct learning pace is essential. For example, reaching the minima could be lengthy if the learning rate needs to be increased. The algorithm needs clarification in this scenario as it repeatedly overshoots the minima due to an excessively high learning rate. It is most effective when the target function is well-behaved and smooth. The issue they're facing is that, if not addressed, it might fail to accomplish their goal.

6.4   Trajectory-Based Algorithms

Following the previous Section 6.3.1, we learned how to formulate an optimization issue systematically. The moment has come to know about optimization algorithms, such as those based on trajectories. As shown in Figure 6.2, the two main categories of *Metaheuristic* algorithms are those that rely on trajectories and those that depend on populations. A single agent iteratively traverses the state search space in a trajectory-based metaheuristic algorithm like *Simulated Annealing*, which is used in artificial intelligence. A better move is always accepted, whereas a not-so-good move can be admitted with a certain probability, as stated in Section (Cf. Section 2.5.2). With a non-zero probability, the moves (steps) trace a route in the search space likely to achieve the global optimum. However, algorithms based on populations, such as *Genetic Algorithms*(Cf. Section 2.5.3), *Ant Colony Optimization*(Cf. Section 2.5.4), and *Particle Swarm Optimization*, employ many agents to

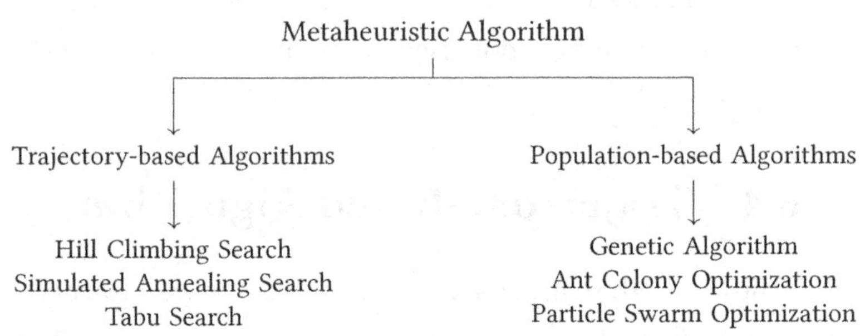

Figure 6.2: Hierarchy of Metaheuristic Algorithm

find the best or nearby solution. These optimization techniques will be valuable for solving complicated optimization issues in various AI contexts.

6.4.1   TBA: Problems to Address

Some trajectory-based optimization techniques in AI, like simulated annealing, hill climbing, tabu search, and others, have problems in different contexts. Let's now examine each issue associated with each algorithm separately. It begins with simulated annealing, an AI metaheuristic search technique for solving optimization issues. The algorithm continuously modifies the answer until it surpasses the computer's current best solution. The system iterates through this procedure until the progress slows down or halts. The main issue with simulated annealing is that we never receive an instant solution when we modify the outcome. Systems typically use this method when they don't need to find a solution immediately because of its laborious nature. Furthermore, fine-tuning the algorithm's parameters might be challenging and produce less-than-ideal outcomes. This Section 2.5.2 covers the comprehensive details of simulated annealing. Simulation annealing has resolved numerous optimization issues, including the traveling salesman problem, ML, the satisfiability problem, and other AI-related issues. The next trajectory-based algorithm is a hill-climbing optimization search, which determines the next step in the state space by combining *DFS* and feedback. Hill climbing search algorithms are characterized by their sensitivity to initial conditions, lack of global exploration, and local optima. It is a local search algorithm that frequently encounters local optima, which are solutions that outperform their immediate neighbors but may not represent the global optimum. Also, the selection of initial solutions plays

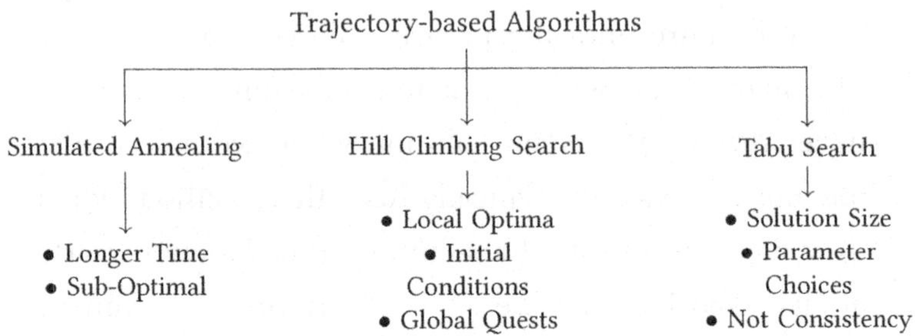

Figure 6.3: Problems with Trajectory-Based Algorithms

an important role. Diverse starting points may result in completely distinct local optima or even unsuccessful convergence. Furthermore, its intrinsic concentration lies in refining the existing solution, perhaps overlooking superior solutions located in remote regions of the search space. The absence of a global exploration mechanism is a critical aspect of determining the global optimum. Section 2.5.1 provides comprehensive information regarding hill-climbing searches. Subsequently, people often conceptualize tabu search as integrating memory structures into local search strategies. Local search aims to tackle numerous issues similar to local optima, as it shares many of the same constraints. For example, it deterministically accepts non-improving solutions (already visited space) to avoid becoming trapped in local minimums. Because these choices and qualities greatly impact Tabu Search's performance, it is typically dependent on them. Furthermore, the size of the solution space and the complexity of the evaluation function can influence a search's effectiveness. Moreover, while tabu searches often produce the best results, selecting appropriate neighborhood structures may not always be easy. Figure 6.3 depicts issues with trajectory-based algorithms, and Section 2.5.5 provides a full explanation of tabu search. These kinds of challenges are generally associated with trajectory-based algorithms. Nonetheless, alternative methods, such as population-based algorithms, may yield superior results.

6.5 Population-Based Algorithms

While trajectory-based algorithms (Cf. Section 6.4) usually employ a single agent to search in a state space environment, population-based algorithms use a multi-agent search to locate the best or near-optimal solutions. Population-based algorithms are subsets of meta-heuristic algorithms that attempt to resolve optimization issues through an iterative process of trial and error. Finding the *fittest* components that will result in an optimal or near-optimal solution to an issue is done systematically. Population-based algorithms aim to efficiently find the best possible solution to a problem by exploring all possible possibilities in the search space. These algorithms boost their chances of discovering the global optimum by keeping and evolving a population of solutions, which helps them avoid being caught in local optima. Standard population-based algorithms include *Genetic Algorithms, Evolutionary Strategies, Particle Swarm Optimization,* and *Ant Colony Optimization.* The method begins with a genetic algorithm, which takes its cues from natural selection. These algorithms manage a pool of potential solutions and use genetic operators such as mutation, selection, and crossover to improve the pool over time. Section 2.5.3 goes into more depth about this algorithm. Drawing inspiration from the cooperative behavior of swarms of animals, another example algorithm is Particle Swarm Optimization. In this algorithm, a population of particles or potential solutions is kept, and they navigate the search space by modifying their position

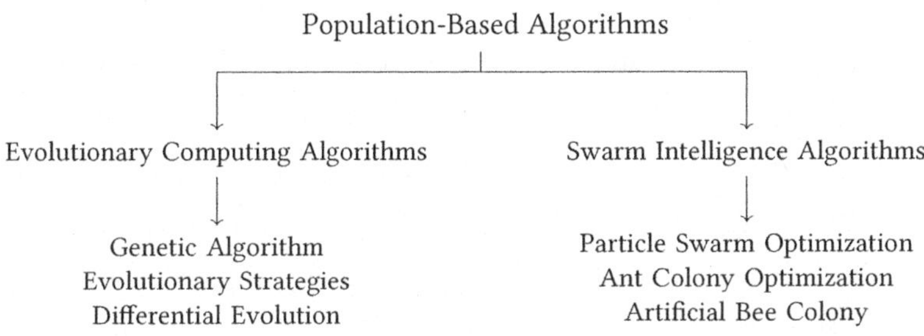

Figure 6.4: Classification for Population-Based Algorithms

and speed according to their own and their neighbors' past experiences. Hence, ant colony optimization takes its cues from ant foraging behavior and applies them to the problem of finding the best route from one location to another by coordinating the actions of a group of artificial ants. There are other explanations for this algorithm under this Section 2.5.4. Finally, evolutionary strategies keep a pool of potential solutions and use variation operators, such as mutation and recombination, to improve the pool over time. Some of the main benefits of algorithms based on populations include better search space exploration, resistance to local optima, and the possibility of finding numerous optimal solutions. All fields, from ML and finance to others, can benefit from their use in resolving complicated optimization problems. Both *Swarm Intelligence* and *Evolutionary Computing* are examples of population-based algorithms. Genetic algorithms and evolutionary techniques are well-liked in the field of evolutionary computing. However, most swarm intelligence population-based methods are particle swarm optimization and ant colony optimization. The following Sections 6.5.1, 6.5.2 elaborate on the issues that need resolving regarding the various types of population-based algorithms, and the Figure 6.4 illustrates these categories.

6.5.1　Evolutionary Computing: Problems to Address

A class of population-based algorithms known as *Evolutionary Computation* algorithms determines the best or nearly the best solution to a given problem. Let's examine a few issues related to evolutionary computation algorithms [WA19], including *Differential Evolution, Evolutionary Strategy,* and *Genetic Algorithms.* It starts with a genetic algorithm. These algorithms could be more effective in resolving specific issues.

Furthermore, it makes no guarantees regarding the caliber of the solution to a particular problem. Additionally, there may be computational difficulties if fitness values are calculated repeatedly. The subsequent evolutionary algorithm is an evolutionary strategy that is computationally costly and requires much larger datasets for learning. Furthermore, the problem could be more efficient when smooth and differentiable. Moreover, it needs more flexibility and takes longer to calculate the best answer. Differential evolution is another form of evolutionary algorithm. For complicated optimization tasks, many function evaluations could be necessary. The accuracy of the measurement is dependent on particular issues. Although it is generally robust for highly multi-modal functions with numerous local optima, it might need help finding the global optimal location. Likewise, it won't offer theoretical assurances of a high-quality solution for a particular issue. Strategies for evolutionary computing are generally more potent and provide an opportunity to use numerous optimization strategies. It may make great strides and become more applicable in resolving complex optimization and decision-making situations in the real

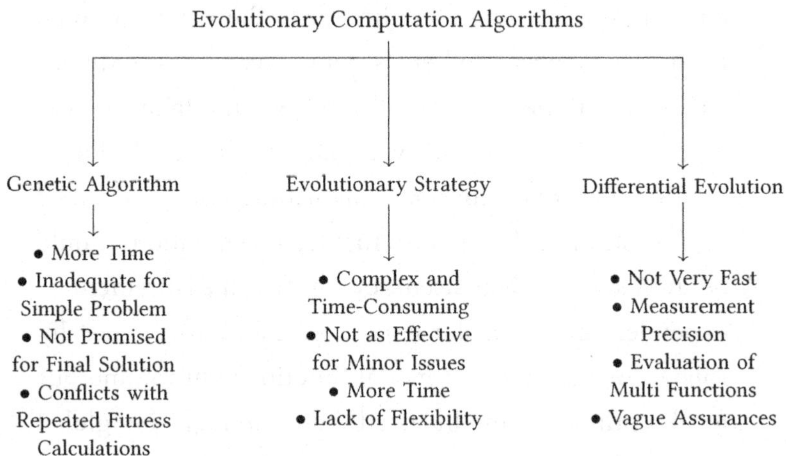

Figure 6.5: Challenges with Evolutionary Computation Algorithms

world by tackling these issues. Figure 6.5 illustrates the problems of the evolutionary computation algorithm in attaining easier comprehension.

6.5.2   Swarm Intelligence: Problems to Address

Population-based algorithms fall within the *Swarm Intelligence Algorithms* category. Let's examine a few issues related to swarm intelligence algorithms, including *Particle Swarm Optimization, Ant Colony Optimization,* and *Artificial Bee Colony* [Ken06]. It begins with particle swarm optimization, a technique that works well but has specific weaknesses. It has a slow rate of iterative convergence and frequently becomes trapped at local optimal points in high-dimensional spaces. The computational cost of directed weighted complex network particle swarm optimization still needs to be improved for particle swarm optimization techniques, even if it is frequently manageable when applied to complex and high-dimensional situations. The next algorithm for swarm intelligence is called ant colony optimization (Cf. Section 2.5.4). The primary issues with an ant colony optimization method include the program's fast shift in convergence speed as the number of iterations increases. Furthermore, the range of values for constants like α and β constitutes a significant portion of the algorithm. Better outcomes need consideration of the appropriate value of α, which is often 1.5. Therefore, regardless of the issue, one should address α for improved results visualization. Furthermore, the solution is quickly caught in an unmodifiable stagnation phase at negative values of α, such as -1.5. This generally applies to situations where there are more ants and fewer cities. Swarm intelligence algorithms can also be classified as artificial bee colonies. Honey bees' clever foraging techniques influenced it. Three key elements comprise the model: food sources, employed bees, and jobless foraging bees. The first two, the working and unemployed foraging bees near their hive, are after the third component, rich food supplies. The model also identifies two leading behaviors required for self-organizing systems and collective intelligence: foragers being drawn to rich food sources, which produces positive feedback, and foragers leaving poor food sources, which produces negative feedback. Artificial bee colony algorithms, which are frequently used for optimization applications, generally mimic the foraging

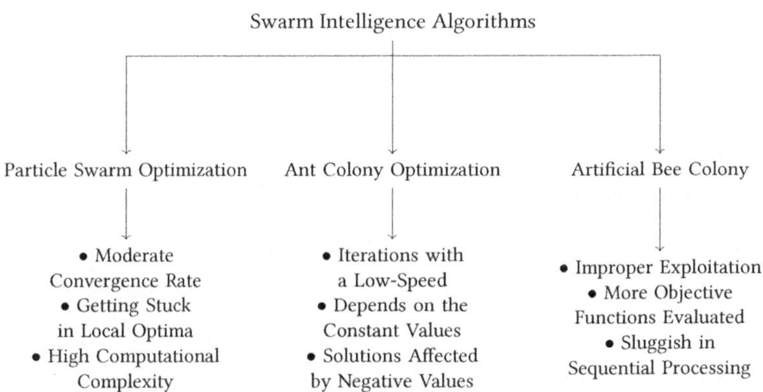

Figure 6.6: Problems with Swarm Intelligence Algorithms

behavior of honeybees. This algorithm has flaws, such as improper application in solving complex problems, a lack of secondary data, the need for additional fitness tests on new algorithm parameters, a higher number of objective function evaluations, and slowness when processing data sequentially. The problems with the swarm intelligence algorithm are illustrated in Figure 6.6 for a better understanding. Overall, complexity and unpredictability are the main issues with swarm intelligence algorithms. This means that emergent behavior in a swarm intelligence algorithm results from the intricate interactions between numerous individual agents; it can be challenging to anticipate or manage. This may complicate the analysis and comprehension of the algorithm's behavior. Parameter sensitivity is another issue, meaning that swarm intelligence algorithms frequently contain several parameters that must be carefully adjusted to attain optimal performance. Selecting the appropriate settings for the parameters can be difficult. Another concern is that swarm intelligence algorithms can identify practical solutions; they only sometimes ensure the global optimum, mainly when dealing with complicated situations. Local optima could trap the algorithm. Furthermore, the emergent behaviors of swarm intelligence algorithms may make it difficult to understand and anticipate systems' reactions in complicated contexts. Overall, there are benefits and drawbacks to population-based algorithms. As a result, it might only be appropriate for some AI challenges. Nevertheless, there are *Machine Learning*-based solutions for these issues, which are covered in Section 6.6.

6.6   Machine Learning Based Algorithms

As previously said, optimization is the iterative process of training a model to achieve a function's most significant or negligible value. It is a fundamental aspect of machine learning that contributes to achieving improved outcomes. It tweaks ML models to enhance their performance and efficiency. Also, it evaluates the outcomes in each iteration by modifying the hyperparameter at each step until it achieves the optimal results. Further, it provides a precise model with a reduced error rate. Various algorithms are available for optimizing a model [YS20], including *Gradient Descent* or GD, *Stochastic Gradient Descent* or SGD, *Mini-batch Gradient Descent* or MGD, *AdaGrad, RMSprop, AdaDelta,* and *Adam.* These algorithms are depicted in the accompanying Figure 6.7. The process begins with gradient descent, a collection of optimization algorithms that iteratively modify the model parameters in the direction opposite to the gradient of the loss function, aiming to reduce the error. The stochastic gradient descent optimization algorithm is a modified version of gradient descent that updates the model parameters using a randomly chosen part of the training data rather than the complete dataset. This approach enhances computational efficiency. The subsequent Section 6.6.2 discusses the algorithm's comprehensive details. Mini-batch gradient descent is an optimization technique that balances grouping gradient descent and SGD. It involves updating the model parameters using a small batch of training instances. Furthermore, the AdaGrad or *Adaptive Gradient* optimization method enhances the traditional GD optimization technique by dynamically adjusting the learning rate, resulting in a more sophisticated and efficient optimization process. RMSprop, also known as *Root Mean Square Propagation,* is a widely used optimization technique that adjusts the learning rate for each parameter by considering the

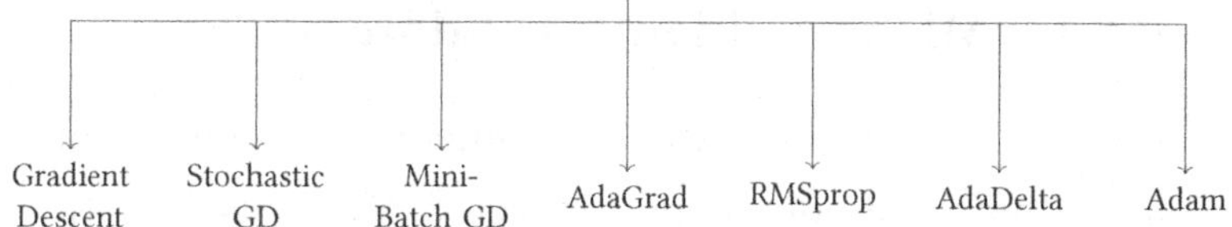

Figure 6.7: Machine Learning-based Common Optimization Algorithms

moving average of the squared gradients. AdaDelta is an extension of AdaGrad that aims to mitigate the issue of the learning rate lowering too rapidly. Additionally, it adjusts the learning rate by considering a limited set of recent gradients instead of summing together all previous squared gradients. Adam, also known as *Adaptive Moment Estimation*, is an optimization technique that calculates adaptive learning rates for each parameter, which makes it particularly effective for situations that involve sparse gradients and noisy problems. In general, selecting an optimization strategy is contingent upon the particular problem, model structure, and dataset properties and is frequently a crucial element of the ML optimization process. The following Section 6.6.1 covers the issues connected with all these common optimization algorithms.

6.6.1 MLA: Problems to Address

Machine learning-based common optimization algorithms present many connected problems [YS20]. Let us begin with the gradient descent optimization algorithm. The primary issues associated with this technique arise when the amount of data points (n) is substantial, resulting in a significant increase in the time required for more iterations (r) to compute the optimal vector. The algorithm has a computational complexity of $\mathscr{O}(rn^2)$. Furthermore, in intricate cost landscapes, GD may become trapped in local minima, mainly when dealing with non-convex optimization issues. The solution to this problem is obtained using the stochastic gradient descent approach. In this context, m represents a randomly picked sample of data from a population of size n. The temporal complexity is expressed as $\mathscr{O}(km^2)$. Therefore, m is considerably smaller than n. Consequently, it has a shorter computational time compared to Gradient Descent. Furthermore, the updates may generate noise as they heavily depend on a solitary example, leading to cost function fluctuations.

Accordingly, the algorithm fails to reach a minimum and moves erratically around the cost landscape. Therefore, accurately adjusting hyper-parameters is essential for this approach. Mini-batch gradient descent also necessitates the selection of an appropriate learning rate for experimentation. Moreover, if the batch size is insufficient, it will encounter the limitations of SGD. In contrast, if the batch size is enormous, it may become susceptible to the problems associated with standard GD. AdaGrad is an optimization algorithm with the following challenges: As the training advances, the sum of squared gradients might increase significantly, resulting in a decrease in learning rates and their eventual reduction to extremely tiny values. This can abruptly terminate the process of acquiring knowledge. The RMSprop optimization technique is employed to address AdaGrad's limitations. It addresses the rapidly declining learning rate in AdaGrad by prioritizing recent gradients, resulting in consistent progress during training. AdaDelta is a machine learning optimization approach that increases the algorithm's complexity by tracking and updating two different state variables for gradients and parameter updates. This can introduce greater complexity in the implementation and comprehension, in contrast to more precise approaches such as SGD. Additionally, it may have a slower

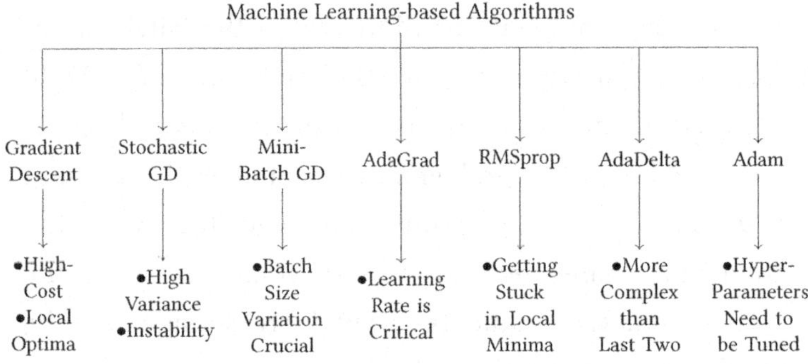

Figure 6.8: Issues with Machine Learning-based Algorithms

convergence rate compared to other optimizers, such as Adam, particularly in scenarios where the learning rate requires more assertive adjustment. The self-regulating learning rate system might occasionally exhibit excessive prudence, resulting in a reduced pace of advancement. Ultimately, the Adam optimization process necessitates the adjustment of hyper-parameters, but it typically performs satisfactorily with the default settings. For better interpretation, Figure 6.8 illustrates the challenges associated with machine learning algorithms. Based on the aforementioned specific concerns, it is evident that non-convexity, large dimensionality, and overfitting pose significant challenges for these algorithms. Although we covered several basic optimization algorithms based on ML, Stochastic Gradient Descent is a popular choice in ML models. As a result of this factor, the following Section 6.6.2 is thoroughly examined.

6.6.2   Stochastic Gradient Descent Algorithm

Stochastic Gradient Descent or SGD, is a widely used and prevalent technique in many ML algorithms [Bot10]. It is the foundation for *Neural Networks*, which are essential for *Deep Learning*. To comprehend SGD, it is necessary to grasp the concept of gradient descent first. As mentioned, SGD exhibits a higher speed than *Gradient Descent* or GD. Let's examine a clear example to illustrate this statement. Suppose we have a two-dimensional equation and three data points. We aim to identify the line that best aligns with these three data points. The equation is represented by $y = mx + c$, where *m* represents the slope and *c* represents the intercept. Therefore, our line must incorporate all these data points for optimal fit. Next, we will assign arbitrary values to the slope and intercept. Assume that the slope is one and the intercept is zero. Consequently, we shall derive the equation of a single line, such as $y = x$. Now that we have a line, we can calculate the loss using a loss function. A loss function is a simple way to assess the algorithm's performance representing a large dataset. If your predictions deviate significantly from the actual values, your loss function will yield a greater numerical value. Conversely, if they are reasonably proficient, it will generate a reduced numerical value. So, we will utilize the sum of squares as the loss function, which is the square of the difference between the actual and predicted data points. Subsequently, we alter the loss function by substituting the predicted value with an equation like $y = x$, as this equation represents the prediction. The complete process is referred to as gradient descent. However, the issue lies in its sluggish performance.

For instance, we had information for 2700 genes and 1 million data points. Hence, there are 1 million terms for each of the 2700 derivatives, resulting in a staggering

27 billion terms for every step. It is typical to perform gradient descent with 1000 iterations. Upon completion of the computation, we will have a total of 27 trillion terms. Henceforth, GD exhibits reduced efficiency when dealing with a substantial amount of data. However, SGD leverages gradient descent and operates similarly, with the distinction that it randomly selects one data point at each step, making it stochastic. One way to improve your SGD model is by implementing mini-batch processing, where SGD uses more than one data point at a time but still fewer than processing the complete dataset at each step of GD. Based on the example, SGD can store up to 1 million terms for 1 million data points. This substantially reduces the amount of data that needs to be processed by the GD algorithm. Therefore, SGD is referred to as a faster Gradient Descent. Additionally, SGD effectively handles new data samples. The SGD technique allows for the seamless integration of fresh data samples at any point throughout the training process, making it a simple task. SGD can do calculations more quickly than GD, batch-GD, or BGD. However, GD will bring you closer to the optimal solution than SGD. Therefore, you are prioritizing speed at the expense of accuracy. If achieving

proximity to the optimal solution is satisfactory, SGD would be the most suitable method. However, employing GD would be recommended if you require more optimal outcomes. The BGD algorithm is between the GD and SGD algorithms. This optimization approach is popular for specific ML and AI problems because of its effectiveness. Despite the optimization challenges faced by various approaches, a *Learning Automaton* can be seen as a system that adjusts its control strategy based on past experiences to achieve optimization. This concept will be further explored in the following Section 6.7.

6.7   Learning Automata-Based Algorithms

Learning Automata, or LA, is a machine learning algorithm that determines its current behavior by considering past experiences gained from the environment [Kor+21]. Furthermore, it will be classified within the domain of the *Reinforcement Learning* paradigm. A *Markov Decision Process*, or MDP, is employed if the environment is random. MDP refers to a form of stochastic process wherein the future outcomes of decisions rely on the system's current state in a probabilistic manner. MDPs are utilized in situations that include sequential decision-making, where it is crucial to consider the ramifications of previous conclusions to make more informed decisions in the future. LA is an adaptive decision-making entity in a stochastic environment that acquires knowledge of the best action by engaging in repeated interactions with its environment. The actions are selected based on a predefined probability distribution, which is adjusted according to the automaton's perception of the environment's response to its actions. In the discipline of reinforcement learning, LA is defined as policy iterators. Policy iterators differ from conventional reinforcement learners in that they directly change the policy. Similarly, *Evolutionary Algorithms* performed the identical task. As previously said, optimization problems pose a significant challenge to AI. Analytical approaches are generally only suitable for some practical applications. Nevertheless, numerical methods such as evolutionary algorithms and learning-automata-based methods address such difficulties as estimating global optima. Several approaches are prone to converging to local optima and have a slow convergence rate. LA has been utilized to improve the outcomes. Several optimization methods based on LA are accessible, including fundamental ones like *Harmony Search, Butterfly Optimization,* and *Grey Wolf Optimization,* as shown in Figure 6.9. A meta-heuristic optimizer named

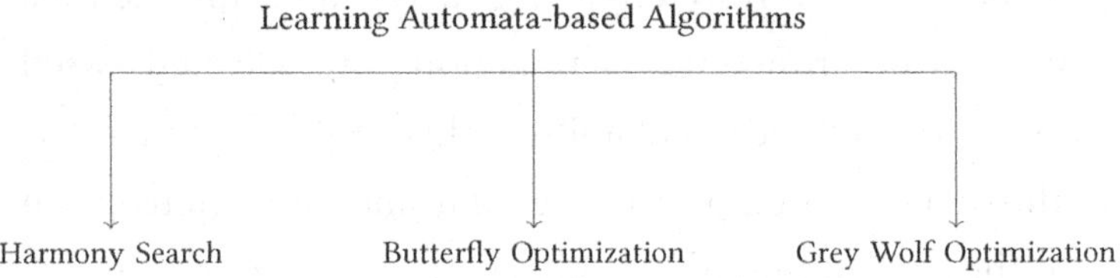

Figure 6.9: Learning Automata-based Basic Optimization Algorithms

Harmony Search, or HS, draws inspiration from musical improvisation. During music improvisation, a specific group of musicians strives to adjust the pitch of their instruments to achieve a harmonious and optimal state. The unique correlation between many sound waves with varying frequencies characterizes harmony in nature. The aesthetic evaluation determines the quality of the improvised harmony. Musicians engage in repeated practice sessions to enhance the aesthetic evaluation and achieve optimal harmony. There are parallels between the improvisation techniques musicians use and the optimization procedures. The primary purpose of an optimization issue is to identify the global optimum of the objective function by adjusting a predetermined set of choice factors. In an optimization problem, the choice variables form a solution vector. Next, the choice variables are inserted into the objective function, and the solution vector's quality is evaluated. The solution vector is iteratively updated until the global optimum is achieved. The Butterfly Optimization Algorithm, or BOA, is a metaheuristic algorithm based on butterflies' natural foraging behavior. Butterflies release a scent while they are searching for food. The released scent not only aids butterflies in locating food but also in recognizing a potential mate. BOA can conduct both local and global searches. The Grey Wolf Optimizer, or GWO, is a successful and widely recognized meta-heuristic algorithm. It replicates the hierarchical structure of hunting behavior observed in grey wolves in their natural environment. Four distinct categories of grey wolves, namely alpha, beta, delta, and omega, are utilized to simulate the hierarchical structure of leadership. Furthermore, the optimization process involves three primary stages: locating prey, surrounding prey, and capturing prey. This Section 6.7.1 addresses the problems related to these LA-based basic optimization techniques.

6.7.1 LA: Problems to Address

The previous Section 6.7 introduced three fundamental optimization approaches based on learning automata: Harmony Search, Butterfly Optimization, and Grey Wolf Optimization. Now, let's examine the obstacles they face in the real-world environment, as depicted in Figure 6.10. The Harmony Search or HS method is a well-known metaheuristic algorithm that employs an efficient exploration procedure. Its advantages include reduced algorithm parameters, simple implementation, and seamless integration with other intelligent algorithms. Simultaneously, it also possesses numerous disadvantages. For instance, the algorithm is prone to get stuck in local optima. It necessitates a wide range of starting solution sets and slow convergence speed, resulting in a less effective algorithm development process for discovering the global optimal value. Furthermore, the selection of parameters poses a significant challenge in the HS algorithm. Researchers

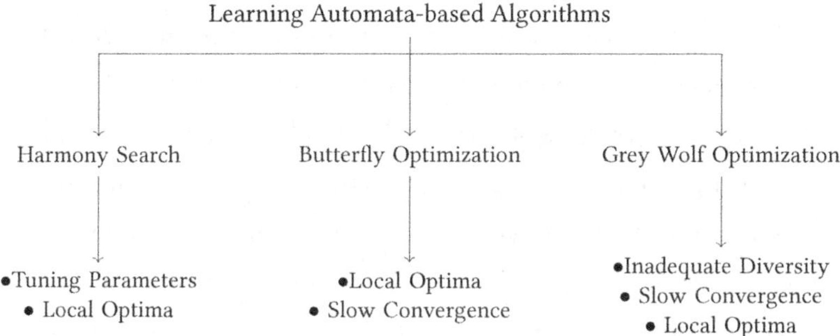

Figure 6.10: Issues with Learning Automata-based Optimization Algorithms

utilized learning automata to effectively choose appropriate harmony search criteria and overcome the problems above. Now, let us examine the Butterfly Optimization Algorithm or BOA and the barriers it faces in typical real-world environments. As mentioned, BOA's structure is based on butterflies' natural foraging behavior. Despite its limitations, the BOA algorithm is prone to getting stuck in local optima, resulting in a slow and inefficient convergence rate for handling complex optimization problems. LA is employed to enhance the pace at which global convergence is achieved towards the genuine global optimum while maintaining the fundamental characteristics of the BOA. Let us examine the barriers to applying Grey Wolf Optimization or GWO to real-world applications. The GWO algorithm draws inspiration from wolf packs' hierarchical structure and hunting behavior. As previously mentioned, this method is commonly employed due to its clarity. However, it exhibits a sluggish convergence rate, limited ability to explore local solutions, and can become trapped in a local minimum for specific situations. The GWO incorporates learning automata to acquire knowledge of the objective function and determine whether it is unimodal or multimodal. An unimodal function requires effective exploitation of potential regions within the search space. Nevertheless, the multimodal function necessitates a high level of exploratory capability. The categorization acquired using LA is, after that, utilized to generate novel solutions within the relevant domains. These are the various approaches that the LA employs to address complicated real-world situations.

6.8 Summary

This chapter begins by introducing the fundamental notion of artificial intelligence optimization. After that, optimization methods, including deterministic, trajectory-based, population-based, and machine-learning-based algorithms, are described in this chapter. It also discusses the issues associated with these algorithms. Lastly, this chapter finishes by providing an overview of learning automata-based optimization techniques and the difficulties they provide. AI systems can simplify and obtain optimal solutions by utilizing optimization problems. Overall, AI-based optimization algorithms are continuously growing and developing. It is our responsibility to utilize this knowledge. Moreover, an extensive range of abilities effectively addresses current issues and actively influences the future.

6.8.1 Multiple Choice Questions

Exercise 1: Which of the following is the objective of an optimization?

a) To achieve learning within limits

b) To achieve an optimal solution within specific constraints

c) To achieve learning without limits

d) To reach the current state with the help of past experience

Exercise 2: What is the purpose of deterministic optimization in AI?

a) To find the global optimal solution

b) To achieve machine learning objectives

c) To reach the current state with the help of past experience

d) To achieve learning with some constraints

Exercise 3: Which of the following is a trajectory-based algorithm?

a) Depth-first search

b) Breadth-first search

c) Simulated annealing search

d) Bidirectional search

Exercise 4: Which of the following is a population-based algorithm?

a) Depth-first search   b) Breadth-first search

c) Simulated annealing   d) Particle swarm
search   optimization

Exercise 5: Which trajectory-based algorithms do not provide consistent solutions?

a) Simulated annealing   b) Tabu search

c) Hill climbing   d) Iterated local search

Exercise 6: Which of the following is not an evolutionary computation algorithm?

a) Genetic algorithm   b) Evolutionary strategy

c) Differential evolution   d) Artificial bee colony

Exercise 7: Which of the following is not a swarm intelligence algorithm?

a) Artificial bee colony   b) Ant colony
optimization

c) Particle swarm   d) Genetic algorithm
optimization

Exercise 8: AdaDelta is an extension of AdaGrad. State whether it is true or false.

a) True

b) False

Exercise 9: Which of the following does not fall under a machine learning-based optimization algorithm?

a) Stochastic gradient descent

b) Gradient Descent

c) AdaDelta

d) Ant colony optimization

Exercise 10: Which of the following machine learning-based optimization algorithms needs to improve hyper-parameters?

a) Mini-batch gradient descent

b) RMSprop

c) Adam

d) AdaDelta

Exercise 11: Suppose the AI environment uses stochastic and markov decision-making processes. Which of the following categories does the learning automata fall under?

a) Supervised learning

b) Reinforcement learning

c) Unsupervised learning   d) Ensemble learning

Exercise 12: Which of the following optimization algorithms draws inspiration from musical improvisation?

a) Grey wolf optimization   b) Harmony search

c) Butterfly optimization   d) Ant colony optimization

6.8.2 Short Answer Type Questions

1. Define optimization and list its advantages.

2. Identify the four components of formulating an optimization problem.

3. Define the trajectory-based algorithms and how they differ from population-based ones.

4. Enumerate four issues associated with the genetic algorithm method.

5. Identify any four challenges associated with the artificial bee colony algorithm.

6. What is the difference between gradient descent
   and stochastic gradient descent?

7. Outline learning automata and enumerate its
   benefits.

8. List all the problems using the grey wolf
   optimization technique.

9. Explain the differences between harmony search
   and butterfly search optimization.

10. How can learning automata be used to solve
    challenging optimization problems? Give any four
    justifications.

6.8.3   Long Answer Type Questions

1. Give a brief explanation of the issues with
   deterministic optimization strategies.

2. Discuss the different types of trajectory-based
   algorithms in optimization problems with suitable
   examples.

3. Examine the different types of population-based
   algorithms in optimization problems with suitable

examples.

4. Provide explanations of the standard optimization algorithms based on machine learning and use appropriate examples.

5. Describe the stochastic gradient descent algorithm using appropriate instances.

6. Analyze the different types of learning automata-based optimization algorithms with suitable examples.

7. Briefly describe the challenges and solutions of learning automata optimization techniques.

Appendix A

Hot Research Topics

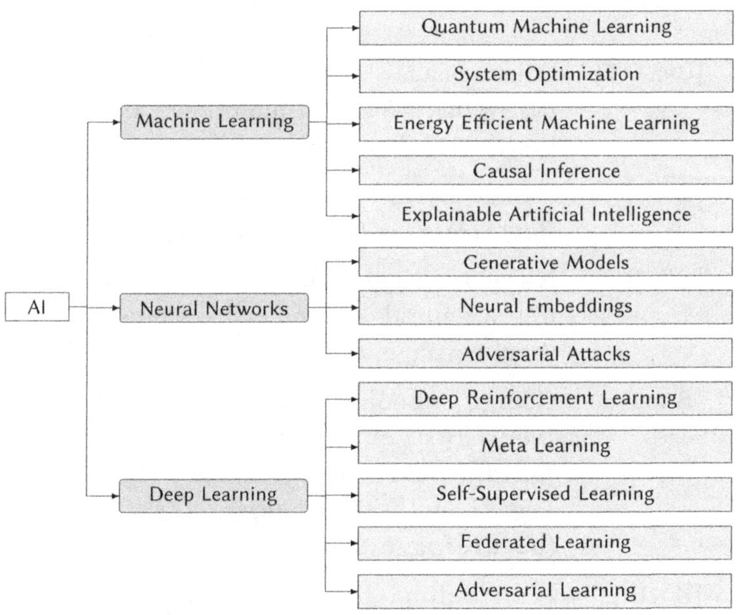

Figure A.1: AI: Hot Research Topics

Bibliography

[Baa+17]   Franz Baader **andothers**. *Introduction to description logic*. Cambridge University Press, 2017 (**backrefpage** 202).

[Ber19]   Daniel Berrar. *Bayes' theorem and naive Bayes classifier* (2019) (**backrefpage** 199).

[Big93]   Norman Biggs. *Algebraic graph theory*. 67. Cambridge university press, 1993 (**backrefpage** 94).

[Boo21]   George Boole. *An Investigation of the Laws of Thought on which are founded the mathematical theories of Logic and Probabilities (1854)* (2021) (**backrefpage** 195).

[Bot10]   Léon Bottou. *Large-scale machine learning with stochastic gradient descent*. Proceedings of COMPSTAT'2010: 19th International Conference on Computational StatisticsParis France, August 22-27, 2010 Keynote, Invited and Contributed Papers. Springer. 2010, **pages** 177–186 (**backrefpage** 277).

[Bro11]   Jason Brownlee. *Clever algorithms: nature-inspired programming recipes.* Jason Brownlee, 2011 (**backrefpage** 79).

[BS19]   Noam Brown **and** Tuomas Sandholm. *Superhuman AI for multiplayer poker.* Science 365.6456 (2019), **pages** 885–890 (**backrefpage** 158).

[Cam60]   Donald T Campbell. *Blind variation and selective retentions in creative thought as in other knowledge processes.* Psychological review 67.6 (1960), **page** 380 (**backrefpage** 29).

[Car18]   Lewis Carroll. *What the tortoise said to Achilles.* Thinking about Logic. Routledge, 2018, **pages** 3–7 (**backrefpage** 229).

[CCD]   Pádraig Cunningham, Matthieu Cord **and** Sarah Jane Delany. *Supervised learning.* Machine learning techniques for multimedia: case studies on organization and retrieval. Springer, **pages** 21–49 (**backrefpage** 24).

[Cha+16]   Hyeong Soo Chang **andothers**. *Google DeepMind's AlphaGo: operations research's unheralded role in the path-breaking achievement.* Or/Ms Today 43.5 (2016), **pages** 24–30 (**backrefpage** 151).

[Cha18]   C Aggarwal Charu. *Neural networks and deep learning: a textbook*. Spinger, 2018 (**backrefpage** 37).

[ČLM13]   Matej Črepinšek, Shih-Hsi Liu **and** Marjan Mernik. *Exploration and exploitation in evolutionary algorithms: A survey*. ACM computing surveys (CSUR) 45.3 (2013), **pages** 1–33 (**backrefpage** 80).

[Don+20]   Xibin Dong **andothers**. *A survey on ensemble learning*. Frontiers of Computer Science 14 (2020), **pages** 241–258 (**backrefpage** 34).

[Dor92]   Marco Dorigo. *Optimization, learning and natural algorithms*. Ph. D. Thesis, Politecnico di Milano (1992) (**backrefpage** 83).

[End01]   Herbert B Enderton. *A mathematical introduction to logic*. Elsevier, 2001 (**backrefpage** 165).

[Ert18]   Wolfgang Ertel. *Introduction to artificial intelligence*. Springer, 2018 (**backrefpage** 61).

[Flo13]   Christodoulos A Floudas. *Deterministic global optimization: theory, methods and applications*. **volume** 37. Springer Science & Business Media, 2013 (**backrefpages** 253, 254).

[For79]   Charles Lanny Forgy. *On the efficient implementation of production systems.* Carnegie Mellon University, 1979 (**backrefpage** 232).

[For89]   Charles L Forgy. *Rete: A fast algorithm for the many pattern/many object pattern match problem.* Readings in artificial intelligence and databases. Elsevier, 1989, **pages** 547–559 (**backrefpage** 233).

[FT91]   Drew Fudenberg **and** Jean Tirole. *Game theory.* MIT press, 1991 (**backrefpage** 117).

[Glo89]   Fred Glover. *Tabu search—part I.* ORSA Journal on computing 1.3 (1989), **pages** 190–206 (**backrefpage** 88).

[GP07]   Ben Goertzel **and** Cassio Pennachin. *Artificial general intelligence.* **volume** 2. Springer, 2007 (**backrefpage** 9).

[Heu19]   Manuel Heusner. "Search behavior of greedy best-first search". phdthesis. University_of_Basel, 2019 (**backrefpage** 63).

[HNR68]   Peter E Hart, Nils J Nilsson **and** Bertram Raphael. *A formal basis for the heuristic determination of minimum cost paths.* IEEE transactions on Systems Science and Cybernetics 4.2 (1968), **pages** 100–107 (**backrefpage** 67).

[Hoc87]   Herbert Hochberg. *Russell's early analysis of relational predication and the asymmetry of the predication relation.* Philosophia 17 (1987), **pages** 439–459 (**backrefpage** 196).

[Hol92]   John H Holland. *Genetic algorithms.* Scientific american 267.1 (1992), **pages** 66–73 (**backrefpage** 80).

[HW62]   David H Hubel **and** Torsten N Wiesel. *Receptive fields, binocular interaction and functional architecture in the cat's visual cortex.* The Journal of physiology 160.1 (1962), **page** 106 (**backrefpage** 26).

[Jam07]   William James. *The principles of psychology.* **volume** 1. Cosimo, Inc., 2007 (**backrefpage** 21).

[Ken06]   James Kennedy. *Swarm intelligence.* Handbook of nature-inspired and innovative computing: integrating classical models with emerging technologies. Springer, 2006, **pages** 187–219 (**backrefpage** 267).

[KM75]   Donald E Knuth **and** Ronald W Moore. *An analysis of alpha-beta pruning.* Artificial intelligence 6.4 (1975), **pages** 293–326 (**backrefpage** 115).

[Kor+21]   Javidan Kazemi Kordestani **andothers**. *Advances in Learning Automata and*

Intelligent Optimization. Springer, 2021 (**backrefpage** 280).

[Kow74]   Robert Kowalski. *Predicate logic as programming language.* IFIP congress. **volume** 74. 1974, **pages** 569–544 (**backrefpage** 212).

[Law63]   Reed C Lawlor. *What computers can do: Analysis and prediction of judicial decisions.* American Bar Association Journal (1963), **pages** 337–344 (**backrefpage** 6).

[LV12]   Kanal Leveen **and** Kumar Vipin. *Search in artificial intelligence.* Springer Science & Business Media, 2012 (**backrefpages** 45, 67).

[Mac05]   Danielle Macbeth. *Frege's logic.* Harvard University Press, 2005 (**backrefpage** 196).

[Mal13]   Marko Malink. *Aristotle's modal syllogistic.* Harvard University Press, 2013 (**backrefpage** 212).

[Min12]   Jack Minker. *Logic-based artificial intelligence.* **volume** 597. Springer Science & Business Media, 2012 (**backrefpage** 193).

[Min61]   Marvin Minsky. *Steps toward artificial intelligence.* Proceedings of the IRE 49.1 (1961), **pages** 8–30 (**backrefpage** 6).

[Min88]   Marvin Minsky. *Society of mind.* Simon **and** Schuster, 1988 (**backrefpage** 15).

[Mit79]   Tom Michael Mitchell. *Version spaces: an approach to concept learning.* Stanford University, 1979 (**backrefpage** 21).

[Moo03]   James Moor. *The Turing test: the elusive standard of artificial intelligence.* **volume** 30. Springer Science & Business Media, 2003 (**backrefpage** 11).

[Nik+54]   Hukukane Nikaidô **andothers**. *On von Neumann's minimax theorem.* Pacific J. Math 4.1 (1954), **pages** 65–72 (**backrefpage** 115).

[Nil82]   Nils J Nilsson. *Principles of artificial intelligence.* Springer Science & Business Media, 1982 (**backrefpages** 47, 50, 52, 55).

[NSS59]   Allen Newell, John C Shaw **and** Herbert A Simon. *Report on a general problem solving program.* IFIP congress. **volume** 256. Pittsburgh, PA. 1959, **page** 64 (**backrefpage** 9).

[Pat13]   Günther Patzig. *Aristotle's theory of the syllogism: A logico-philological study of book A of the prior analytics.* **volume** 16. Springer Science & Business Media, 2013 (**backrefpage** 195).

[RD06]   Matthew Richardson **and** Pedro Domingos. *Markov logic networks.* Machine learning 62 (2006), **pages** 107–136 (**backrefpage** 199).

[RN16]   Stuart J Russell **and** Peter Norvig. *Artificial intelligence: a modern approach.* Pearson, 2016 (**backrefpage** 103).

[Sam59]   Arthur L Samuel. *Some studies in machine learning using the game of checkers.* IBM Journal of research and development 3.3 (1959), **pages** 210–229 (**backrefpage** 144).

[SB06]   Aleksander Sadikov **and** Ivan Bratko. *Pessimistic heuristics beat optimistic ones in real-time search.* Frontiers in Artificial Intelligence and Applications 141 (2006), **page** 148 (**backrefpage** 116).

[SG06]   Bart Selman **and** Carla P Gomes. *Hill-climbing search.* Encyclopedia of cognitive science 81 (2006), **page** 82 (**backrefpage** 73).

[Sil+16]   David Silver **andothers**. *Mastering the game of Go with deep neural networks and tree search.* nature 529.7587 (2016), **pages** 484–489 (**backrefpage** 150).

[SK89]   Anton Scheucher **and** Hermann Kaindl. *The Reason for the Benefits of Minimax Search.* IJCAI. Citeseer. 1989, **pages** 322–327 (**backrefpage** 116).

[Tur50]   Alan Mathison Turing. *Mind.* Mind 59.236 (1950), **pages** 433–460 (**backrefpage** 5).

[Van+87]   Peter JM Van Laarhoven **andothers**. *Simulated annealing*. Springer, 1987 (**backrefpage** 76).

[Van91]   Eric Van Damme. *Stability and perfection of Nash equilibria*. **volume** 339. Springer, 1991 (**backrefpage** 154).

[VW12]   Martijn Van Otterlo **and** Marco Wiering. *Reinforcement learning and markov decision processes*. Reinforcement learning: State-of-the-art. Springer, 2012, **pages** 3–42 (**backrefpage** 29).

[WA19]   Gai-Ge Wang **and** Amir H Alavi. *Evolutionary computation*. MDPI, 2019 (**backrefpage** 264).

[YS20]   Li Yang **and** Abdallah Shami. *On hyperparameter optimization of machine learning algorithms: Theory and practice*. Neurocomputing 415 (2020), **pages** 295–316 (**backrefpages** 271, 274).

[Zad96]   Lotfi A Zadeh. *Fuzzy logic= computing with words*. IEEE transactions on fuzzy systems 4.2 (1996), **pages** 103–111 (**backrefpage** 200).

[ZG22]   Xiaojin Zhu **and** Andrew B Goldberg. *Introduction to semi-supervised learning*. Springer Nature, 2022 (**backrefpage** 28).

[Zob90]   Albert L Zobrist. *A new hashing method with application for game playing*. ICGA Journal 13.2 (1990), **pages** 69–73 (**backrefpage** 148).

Made in the USA
Monee, IL
07 July 2026